how2become

How to Become an Offshore Worker

www.How2Become.com

Orders: Please contact How2Become Ltd, Suite 3, 40 Churchill Square Business Centre, Kings Hill, Kent ME19 4YU.

You can order through Amazon.co.uk under ISBN: 9781912370573, via the website www.How2Become.com or through Gardners.com.

ISBN: 9781912370573

First published 2018

Typeset for How2Become Ltd by Gemma Butler.

Disclaimer

Every effort has been made to ensure that the information contained within this guide is accurate at the time of publication. How2Become Ltd is not responsible for anyone failing any part of any selection process as a result of the information contained within this guide. How2Become Ltd and their authors cannot accept any responsibility for any errors or omissions within this guide, however caused. No responsibility for loss or damage occasioned by any person acting, or refraining from action, as a result of the material in this publication can be accepted by How2Become Ltd. The information within this guide does not represent the views of any third party service or organisation.

at is an Offshore Worker?

shore Working, quite literally, means working off the shore. That
> say, you will be working in a place relatively far from land. The
e of tasks and work that you do will depend on the installation
ere you are working, and your role – as will the facilities. However,
e are certain things which you can expect, including:

Long days, often working 12-hour shifts.

Harsh/rough weather conditions. This is especially the case if
you are working offshore in a location such as the North Sea.

Isolation. You'll be with colleagues and fellow professionals,
of course, but you must be prepared to spend significant time
away from any family or friends.

Helicopter travel. In order to get to and from the offshore facility,
vorkers will often travel via helicopter.

Illy, there will be around 100 other men and women working
e installation with you, at the same time – a full crew. Although
ore installations have a reputation for being uncomfortable
s, this is actually not the case for most. The majority of
ore installations offer a good standard of living for the crew,
en-suite (shared) quarters, and food. However, you should
mber that in pretty much every single reputable installation,
ol is banned. The majority of installations also provide facilities
orkers to exercise, watch videos, or play games. Basically,
s a wide range of facilities available to keep workers occupied
lieve tension and stress. Most installations have a designed
ng team, who will deal with areas such as cleaning, washing
oking. This means that once your shift is over, you can relax
wind.

ork you are doing will of course depend on your exact
ut these days more and more offshore jobs are aided by
logy. This means that there's less manual labour to do, and
echnology focused/monitoring work.

s of shift patterns, the normal pattern for offshore crews is to

CONTENTS

Hello, and welcome to your guide on How To Become An Offshore Worker. In this guide we are going to take you through the process of gaining a job on an Offshore Rig. Whether you are experienced or completely new to the role, want to work in oil, gas, or wind, our top tips are sure to get you over the line, and help you secure your job.

The Structure of This book

The aim of this book is to provide you with as much information about becoming an offshore worker as possible. With this in mind, we'll be covering a wide variety of topics.

- We'll start off by looking at oil, gas and wind farms, and then look at some of the key roles available for aspiring candidates, along with some of the job requirements.

- Following this, we'll look at some potential routes into working offshore, such as apprenticeships, and graduate entry.

- We'll then show you how to find a job as an offshore worker without any prior experience, applying as a roustabout.

- After this, we'll cover some entry tests, application form advice, and interview skills.

In this book, we'll also give you an insight into the core competencies required for offshore workers, which will be invaluable when applying for a job.

How To Use This Guide

The tips contained within this book will be applicable to a wide variety of offshore roles. Whether you are an experienced specialist, or simply looking for an entry level position, our guidance should give you a leg up in the selection process and help you to impress the company that you are applying to.

So, without further ado, let's get started.

What is an Offshore Worker?

W

Of
is
typ
wh
the

-

-

-

-

Usu
on th
offsh
plac
offsh
with
reme
alco
for w
there
and r
cater
and c
and u

The
role,
techn
more

In terr

work for periods of 2-4 weeks, before then heading back to land and resting for two weeks. So, two weeks working, two weeks resting, etc. This means that offshore workers get to spend time with their family and friends on a two-week basis – not so bad when you think about it. Occasionally you might be asked to attend further training whilst 'off duty' but this will be done on land, and only within your means.

Nowadays, offshore installation managers recognise that it's essential to protect the mental and physical wellbeing of their workers, and therefore offshore installations are much more employee friendly than they used to be.

Of course, working offshore does come with its downsides. You must be someone who can co-operate in a group. So, if you think that working offshore means working in isolation and loneliness, think again! It's essential that you can cooperate and get along with the crew. However, for the majority of people, it will be very difficult spending that much time away from family and friends, and therefore it's fair to say that working offshore is not for everyone.

Core Competencies

As with any job, in any industry, offshore workers must adhere to a set of job-specific core competencies. Core competencies are essentially a set of behavioural guidelines for employees to follow. They outline the expectations of the company, and also form a very important part of the application process. This is even more essential when working on an offshore rig, where correct safety procedures are absolutely integral. When you go through the application process, you'll be expected to demonstrate these competencies throughout.

There are a huge number of roles available on offshore rigs. With this in mind, it would be impossible to give you a set of competencies that cover every single position. However, below we have provided you with a basic/general guideline of the types of behaviours that you'll be expected to show – regardless of your position. All of these competencies are really important, and knowing them will be extremely useful during the selection process.

Discipline

Working on an offshore rig requires tremendous discipline. The bottom line is that life on an offshore rig is extremely tough, regardless of what role you are performing. This means that you will need to exercise tremendous discipline. Not just self-discipline, to keep yourself motivated and positive, but discipline in general – adhering to safety regulations, keeping your working standards extremely high, and helping everyone around you to do the same. Discipline is more of a mental strength than physical, you need to have self-belief in your ability to perform the job, and to sustain a good level of performance for the duration of your time on the rig.

A person with good discipline can:

- Keep themselves and others motivated, through good times and bad.

- Maintain a high standard of performance, regardless of the situation they find themselves in.

- Manage their time effectively and efficiently.

- Take an organised approach to their work.

- Understand their own limits, and ask for help when required.

Leadership

Leadership is a very important quality for an offshore worker to have. You might think 'I'm not a leader', but it's not really about 'leading people' as such. It's more about taking responsibility and ownership of situations, being calm, collected, and in control. You don't have to be a great motivator or speaker to work on an offshore rig, but you must be someone who can encourage and **lead by example.** Leading by example means behaving in a way that others could look to, as an example of how to behave. It means demonstrating the core behavioural requirements and expectations of the contractor, in a way that others can aspire to. Of course, being an actual leader – in the traditional sense, is very much welcomed. As we'll explain, teamwork is essential when working on an offshore rig, so your ability to take charge of others and lead them to completing a high standard of work will be really helpful, and especially relevant if you are working as a driller.

A person with good leadership can:

- Remain calm and controlled in the face of adversity.

- Lead by example, acting as a model representative of the contractor.

- Encourage others to maintain their discipline and positivity.

- Help others to complete tasks, offering them advice when needed.

- Develop a relationship with colleagues, to the extent that they can rely on you and trust you.

Mechanical Knowledge

Mechanical knowledge is an extremely useful competency for any offshore worker to have. Working on an offshore rig is generally a very mechanically intensive job. You'll have to work with lots of different types of machinery, depending on the role that you are doing, and will need to have a full understanding of how to use this machinery. Lots of the work you'll be doing whilst on board an offshore facility involves fixing different pieces of equipment, and ensuring that they are running to full capacity. You'll need to have a good understanding of mechanics and physics to do this, with certain roles being more mechanically intensive than others. Health and safety is obviously a huge emphasis here. Most of the equipment that you'll need to use whilst working on an offshore rig is incredibly dangerous, and therefore it's fundamental that you can use this equipment responsibly and in adherence with the correct protocols. Every single person who works on an offshire rig will undergo extensive safety training, to make sure they are up to speed with the requirements.

A person with good mechanical knowledge can:

- Understand the specific needs and requirements for working with different pieces of equipment/machinery.

- Demonstrate a good understanding of physics and mechanics.

- Understand all of the health and safety protocols surrounding the equipment you are using.

- Act responsibility when using dangerous/specialised equipment.

Organisation

Organisation is extremely important when working on an offshore rig. You will be required to perform multiple tasks, to the highest possible standard, and for this reason it's essential that you are organised and working to the best of your ability. You need to have a good understanding of time management, what needs to be done, and when it needs to be done. Furthermore, it's important that you are a flexible person. When you are working on an offshore rig, things can change very quickly. Your priorities might change mid-shift, and you must have the ability to roll with these changes and still produce a high standard of work. The more organised you are, the better work you can produce, because you'll know how and when things need to be finished, and what's coming next, rather than operating in a state of flux – where you don't know what the next task is or how long it will take to complete. Offshore rigs operate on a strict time schedule, almost military like, so you need to be aware of this and organise yourself to accommodate for it.

A person with good organisation can:

- Manage their time effectively and efficiently.

- Rearrange their priorities, to accommodate for changes.

- Work to a strict time schedule, whilst still producing the highest standard of work.

- Understand the value of time management.

- Organise their tasks and priorities in a way that leads to the best possible outcome.

Physical Fitness

There's no getting around it, working on an offshore rig is an extremely physically demanding role. Even though more and more offshore rigs are becoming 'mechanised' these days, there's still an awful lot of physical work to be done, and for this reason you will need to be in good shape. Being in good physical shape means that you can increase the efficiency and quality of your work tenfold. Good physical fitness is also strongly linked with your mental stability.

A person with good physical fitness can:

- Work to a high standard throughout the day, without becoming overwhelmed or exhausted.

- Understand their own physical limits, and how to pace their fitness throughout the day.

- Be capable of performing a wide variety of physical based tasks, including lifting, pushing, and pulling.

- Take steps to improve and maintain their physical fitness, throughout their time on the rig, and whilst off-duty.

Teamwork

Teamwork is incredibly important when working on an offshore rig. The people around you will be fundamental, and the rig can't run successfully without coordination. Many of the tasks performed on an offshore rig will require at least two people acting cohesively, especially given the safety requirements. Therefore, it's vital that you can work as a unit, and get along with the other people on the rig. Remember that you will be effectively living with these people for 2 to 3 weeks at a time, so if you can't get along with them then it's going to be really difficult. Teamwork comes with a variety of different elements, including leadership, communication (our next competency), and emotional awareness.

A person with good teamwork skills can:

- Work in coordination with their colleagues, to produce high quality results.

- Develop good professional and personal relationships with their colleagues.

- Understand and recognise the importance of teamwork whilst working on an offshore rig.

- Demonstrate empathy towards their colleagues, and take other people's views and opinions into consideration.

- Acknowledge when they need help, and ask for assistance when necessary.

Communication

In line with teamwork, communication is also really important. With all of the safety requirements that come from working on an offshore rig, it's fundamental that you and your colleagues can maintain an open line of communication with each other. Without communication and teamwork, things will very quickly go wrong. Communication isn't just about talking to your colleagues, it's about communicating in the right way. Working on an offshore rig requires particular codes of communication, which you will quickly pick up once you get there.

A person with good communication can:

- Identify when it is appropriate to use certain styles of communication and language;

- Adapt their communication according to the individual(s) being addressed;

- Listen carefully when they are being spoken to, taking note of essential information;

- Influence the behaviour of others in a positive way, using good communication.

- Build a rapport with their colleagues.

Respect for Diversity

Working on an offshore rig will put you in contact with many different types of people, from all different walks of life and backgrounds. This means that, in order for you to work as a cohesive unit, you must be someone who can respect diversity. Discrimination of any kind is absolutely not tolerated on an offshore rig, and is extremely harmful to the group dynamic. You must show a respect and decency towards your colleagues and teammates. The better everyone can get along, the more productive the group will be.

A person with respect for diversity can:

- Respect the values and feelings of people from a diverse range of backgrounds;

- Treat every single person that they meet with the utmost respect and fairness;

- Be diplomatic when dealing with all members of the public;

- Understand the need to be sensitive to differing social, cultural and racial requirements;

- Immediately challenge any inappropriate or discriminatory behaviour.

How To Use These Competencies

When it comes to applying for jobs on an offshore rig, you will need to pass a variety of different stages. Starting with a CV, Cover Letter, or application form, you'll then move on to online tests, an assessment centre, and an interview. Different rigs have different application processes, but ALL of them will require you to have an understanding of the competencies. The competencies should basically be used as a guideline for how you approach the application process. Your responses to application and interview questions should try to incorporate as many of the competencies as possible, using keywords from each competency. The better you can show the employer that you have an understanding of what it takes to work on an offshore rig, the more likely you are to get the job.

Oil, Gas, and Wind Farms

Offshore facilities generally focus on three main areas: Oil, gas or wind. In this chapter, we'll give you an overview of all of these areas, and the way they work. This should act as good preparation for a career offshore, as you'll have a better understanding of exactly how and why things are done.

Offshore Gas

Offshore gas facilities focus on extracting natural gas from below the ocean floor. This is done via drilling. In order to extract gas, the majority of offshore drilling is done around continental shelfs. Offshore drilling platforms are prevalent throughout the world.

Obviously, it's not quite as simple as just drilling into the seabed. The process of locating and extracting gas is very complicated. In order to find the right areas to drill into, companies conduct geological surveys to establish where the gas is present, and the best way to extract it. This is the reason why offshore facilities are built – because the locations where gas can be extracted are so far out from land. Furthermore, the gas reservoirs can be extremely far below sea level, sometimes as deep as 30,000 feet or more. In the event that the drilling needs to be in water that is 1000 meters deep or greater, the drilling is known as 'deepwater drilling'.

Building the offshore platform is no easy task. Offshore platforms are constructed onshore, and then get moved to the drilling site. Obviously, the platforms are gargantuan in size, and this means that moving them is quite a lot of work! Once the platform has been placed in the correct position, and the crew is onboard, work can begin.

Offshore gas drilling, in simple terms, is done by driving extremely long drills into the seabed, until they reach specific gas reservoirs. Then, the workers onboard the platform need to perform something known as tapping. This is essentially where the gas is connected to the platform pumps, without losing any of the gas or releasing it in the ocean in the process. Operators then pump the gas into tanks, which are transported to the shore via a pipeline, or a transportation vessel.

Given the nature of the work, and the location, offshore gas drilling comes with plenty of hazards. Offshore drilling platforms need to take very specific measures to prevent pollution, as any spillage could be disastrous. Although health and safety is absolutely paramount onboard an offshore drilling platform, and there will be countless protocols in place to prevent disaster, the risks are still there. Dealing with gas is dangerous, and the potential for hazards is quite strong – including explosions or ignited gas. For this reason, when applying for jobs on an offshore drilling platform, it's a good idea to emphasise your respect for health and safety, and your level of care for environmental issues.

Offshore Oil

Offshore drilling, similarly to gas drilling, uses extraction techniques to gain access to deposits of oil, underneath the ocean floor. Usually, offshore drilling sites are located on the continental shelf, but with improvements to technology there are more and more offshore oil platforms in varying locations, and further out to sea.

In order to locate oil reservoirs, offshore oil companies use 3D surveys, which scan the seabed, and then send sound waves. These waves produce images, which show where the oil is located.

Offshore oil is an extremely popular field, and today companies have an enormous variety of methods for extracting oil. The equipment available to oil companies means that they are capable of drilling at pretty much any depth. Although oil extraction companies come under heavy amounts of criticism, out of worry for the environment, the facts show that without these companies (and the oil they provide), the world would really struggle. The US consumes over 19 million barrels of oil every single day.

Offshore drilling provides companies with access to untapped reserves, and means that countries around the world can rely on their own reserves of oil, instead of importing or exporting the oil.

Despite this, there are some negatives. Offshore drilling comes with a huge amount of risk, and the accident history of offshore oil is well documented. Whether it's human error or mechanical failure, people have lost their lives whilst working on oil rigs, so the risk is something you need to take into account before pursuing this career.

On top of this, the environmental concerns are not without merit. Poorly run or operated rigs will result in ocean spillages, polluting the water. On top of this, the process of installing an offshore oil rig (and the same for gas) can greatly disrupt the ocean ecology at the site.

Oil-drilling technology is constantly improving, and some rigs combine elements from different models to achieve specific abilities. But in general, the major types of offshore oil rigs include the following:

Drilling Platforms

In general, there are two types of offshore oil and gas drilling platforms, or rigs, as they are known – movable and permanent.

Movable rigs come in many different forms. Below we've listed a few of these:

Drilling Barge

Drilling barges are used for drilling in shallow water, such as lakes or rivers. They are usually transported via tugboat between locations. Drilling barges are generally not suitable for larger bodies of water, such as oceans, where the currents and weather can be quite extreme.

Jack-Up Rig

Jack-up rigs are fairly similar to drilling barges, with the key difference being that these rigs don't float like barges – instead they are moored to the bottom of the water/seabed, using legs. Like drilling barges, jack-up rigs are used in shallow water, as the legs wouldn't be suitable for deeper waters.

Since workers on a jack-up rig are on a platform that's further above water level, the general consensus is that jack-up rigs are slightly safer than drilling barges.

Submersible and Semisubmersible Rigs

Submersible rigs are again designed for shallow water. A submersible rig has two platforms, with two hulls. One of the hulls will have the living quarters for the crew, and a drilling platform, and the other hull will be much lower down, which is designed to help the movement of the rig when going between locations. The bottom hull essentially inflates and deflates when necessary.

Semisubmersible rigs are the most frequent type of offshore drilling rig that you'll see, and can function in deep water. Similarly to submersible rigs, the bottom hull inflates and deflates to aid movement. The difference here is that when the air is released from the lower hull, the rig does not submerge to the seabed, and instead fills with water – which in turn provides the rig with a stable platform. Semisubmersible rigs are held into place via enormous, heavy anchors, which combine with the bottom hull to ensure that the rig is stable. Because of this, semisubmersible rigs can be used in deeper water, and are suitable for harsher weather conditions.

Drillship

A drillship is a large boat, designed to carry drilling platforms to deep-sea environments. Drillships also have their own platforms, on which drilling can be done. Drillships are generally used for deepwater drilling, as they are designed to work in turbulent and difficult conditions. In order to locate reservoirs, drill ships use satellite technology.

Fixed platforms can also take a variety of different forms, including:

Compliant Towers

Compliant towers are essentially a single narrow tower, that is attached to a seafloor foundation. They then extend all the way up onto the platform. The tower is extremely flexible, and therefore it can operate in deeper waters and treacherous conditions, even surviving hurricanes.

Floating Production System

Floating production systems are highly similar to semisubmersible rigs, but they use petroleum production tools, on top of drilling equipment. The platforms are kept stable using large anchors, but they can also utilise the technology used by drillships. In a floating production system, the petroleum is extracted and then transported to production facilities on the platform itself, rather than to onshore sites.

Subsea System

Subsea systems are wells, which are located on the seabed, rather than on the surface. They extract petroleum from the seafloor, then send it back to an existing production platform. This means that one well-placed production platform can take extractions from a number of wells spread out over an area.

Spar Platforms

Spar platforms are the largest offshore platforms available. They are built to survive severe weather, using a large cylinder shape as a stabiliser. The cylinder is tethered to the bottom of the rig via a series of cables.

Offshore Wind

The third most popular form of offshore production, is offshore wind. Offshore wind technology means that wind turbines can be installed on the seabed, where they take advantage of the powerful ocean winds. Even the smallest increases in wind speed can have an enormous impact, with differences of just three mph bringing about energy production of almost double. This is particularly beneficial for coastal areas, where offshore wind farms can help to meet energy demands.

The UK has the world's largest offshore wind market, and according to recent studies accounts for over 35% of offshore wind farming. In 2016, in the UK, wind generated more electricity than coal.

Offshore wind farms are becoming more and more popular. Since they are far more environmentally friendly than oil or gas rigs, wind farms are an important part of the world's battle against climate change and one of the primary ways in which people are utilising renewable energy.

For the most part, offshore wind farms have the same advantages as on land. They are an amazing source of renewable energy, and don't cause pollution or emit greenhouse gases. They benefit from stronger wind speeds than land wind farms. That being said, it is highly expensive to construct wind farms. Despite more robust wind farms being constructed, they are still prone to damage during ocean thunderstorms or hurricanes.

Working on A Wind Farm

The core responsibility of those working on a wind farm, is to keep wind turbine equipment running smoothly and efficiently. This involves testing equipment, making mechanical repairs, and monitoring the performance of the equipment. Your responsibilities could include:

- Finding faults on turbine systems.

- Climbing wind turbine towers, using safety protective gear, to carry out essential repairs.

- Repairing system parts and components.

- Reporting to your site manager.

- Producing reports and paperwork based on the day's activities.

- Monitoring stock.

- Following safety procedures.

Basic Offshore Induction and Emergency Training (BOSIET)

Prior to job application, the majority of employers, for the majority of roles, will ask for you to have taken part in Basic Offshore Induction and Emergency Training (BOSIET).

The BOSIET course provides candidates with basic information and knowledge about offshore installation safety matters, and also gives them an understanding of how emergency response measures are conducted offshore.

Once you've completed the BOSIET course, you will have a strong understanding of the types of hazards that you might encounter whilst working offshore, and the safety management systems which are in place to deal with and prevent these hazards. After you receive your BOSIET certificate, it will be valid for a period of 4 years. If you plan on working offshore beyond that period, you'll need to attend a refresher course, known as Further Offshore Emergency Training (FOET).

OPITO

The BOSIET was created by OPITO – an organisational body which runs courses, with the aim of improving standards across the offshore industry. There is an enormous variety of OPITO courses, including emergency response training. OPITO also provide specialist courses for certain careers, such as gas testing and control room operating.

Course Cost

There is a fee to take part in the BOSIET course, but this cost will largely depend on where you are attending. Some course providers charge up to £1000, but others may charge less than this. As of January 2018, it's possible to take the course online, but you'll still need to attend a training centre to fulfil the practical obligations of the course.

Course Structure

There are four modules in total on the BOSIET course, which utilises both theory and practical teaching methods. The modules are as follows:

-    Safety induction.

-    Firefighting and self-rescue.

-    Helicopter safety and escape.

-    Sea survival, and emergency first aid.

Course participants will also receive Compressed Air Emergency Breathing System training.

Taking The Course

In order to take part in BOSIET, you will need to be physically fit. It's a physically demanding course, which requires you to engage in a wide number of practical activities. These will include:

-    Swimming in water, wearing a life jacket.

-    Putting out fires with fire extinguishers.

-    Performing CPR.

-    Pulling yourself onto a life raft from water.

-    Learning to use an air pocket rebreather system, whilst under the water.

-    Helicopter underwater escape training (very tough!).

-    Crawling over and under objects, in visually difficult conditions.

You can learn more about BOSIET, and how to find a course provider, via the following link:

https://www.opito.com/standard/bosiet

Careers Offshore

In this section, we'll cover some of the careers in the industry, and what responsibilities they involve. You might be surprised to learn that not every role offshore involves working with machinery, or carrying out physical tasks. There are actually an enormous variety of roles, for every type of person.

In our job profiles, we've provided you with a brief overview of the career, the things that employers will normally look for, and some of the key skills required. For almost every single job on this list, you can assume that employers will ask for you to have completed your basic offshore induction and emergency training (BOSIET) and have earned your offshore medical certificate.

Accountant

Accountants play an extremely important role in offshore life. As with any company, it's important for businesses to employ an accountant, who can take care of areas such as financial reports, budgets, forecasts and staff wages. It's especially important for offshore companies to take care of their accounts, because running an offshore rig is so incredibly expensive. There are also very strict tax rules in the oil and gas industry, which companies will need to comply with.

Job Requirements

Naturally this will differ depending on the company you are applying for, but usually you will need the following:

- A degree in finance, or another similar business subject.

- An accountancy qualification, such as CIMA or ACCA.

- Companies will generally look for someone who has previous experience of working in an accounting or finance role, or at the very least financial experience with the industry.

Skillset

- You must be a great communicator.

- You must be good at multi-tasking.

- You must be able to adapt to new surroundings.

- You must be competent with numbers and maths.

Administration

 Administrators play a vital role in work on an offshore rig. They are prevalent in both technical and non-technical areas, and perform a lot of the ground work which keeps matters on a rig ticking over. There is a huge variety of administration tasks which need to be performed on an offshore facility, including:

- Creating and maintaining data spreadsheets and reports.

- Cataloguing expenses, invoices and purchase orders.

- Handling the facility's phoneline.

- Arranging meetings and ensuring that the right measures are in place for the meet to run successfully and punctually.

- Maintaining a record of staff holiday/sick leave.

- Ensuring technical training and safety manuals are up to date and available for staff.

In essence, administrators provide essential support to managers onboard offshore platforms. Managing information, even if it might seem benign, is incredibly important to the productive and efficient running of an offshore facility.

Job Requirements

Depending on the position you are applying for, companies might ask for you to have a HNC/HND in either administration, or a business-related subject.

Skillset

- Good organisation.

- Good attention to detail, and a high level of accuracy.

- Good communication skills.

Cementer

Cementers play an essential role in offshore operations, and can also work on land installations. The role of the cementer is essentially to help develop and then pump cement into the wellbore. They are an integral part of the process of preparing a well for drilling. As a cementer, there are a wide variety of tasks which you'll be required to do, including:

- Preparing the slurry for pumping.

- Ensuring that equipment is pressure-tested prior to use.

- Performing essential cementing calculations.

- Making sure that all equipment is operated according to the correct safety procedures and standards.

- Conducting frequent safety checks of the operations area, to ensure the health and safety of co-workers/colleagues.

Job Requirements

Usually, employers will ask for you to have at the very least a Maths and English GCSE, and a HNC in engineering or another related field. Most employers will require you to obtain a Commercial Operators Licence prior to employment. In the interview, you can expect to be quizzed on your general knowledge of drilling techniques and operations, and your equipment operation experience.

Skillset

- You must be someone who is willing to take leadership of situations.

- You must be able to adhere to health and safety standards.

- You must be able to recognise problems/potential problems, and take responsibility for fixing them.

Chemical Process Engineer

 Chemical process engineers play an important role in constructing, and improving, offshore facilities. Since working with oil and gas requires a great deal of chemical knowledge and expertise, it's vital for companies to have experts at hand. Process engineers don't just work on the rigs themselves, but also work at production facilities, and on shore sites, where the oil and gas is stored and processed. As a chemical process engineer, your tasks will include:

- Carrying out routine studies and checks of the production process, to establish where improvements can be made.

- Playing an active role in design and engineering work.

- Conducting risk assessments.

- Providing technical expertise and knowledge.

Job Requirements

You will need a degree in Chemical Engineering to gain this role. Along with this, companies will usually look for someone with work experience in a similar field. Companies will look for someone willing to improve and progress, and you'll need to be willing to take a lot of safety training before you can start.

Skillset

- You must be a great team worker.

- You must be an analytical person, with an ability to solve problems.

- You must be dedicated to the health and safety of your colleagues.

- You must be an open minded and flexible person.

Completions Engineer

 The role of a completions engineer is essentially to manage offshore projects – ensuring that the installation of wells is done efficiently and smoothly, and helping oil and gas production to function as intended. Completions engineers are also based onshore, where there are a variety of places that can make the most of their skillset. Much of working as a completions engineer is project-management focused. Your tasks will include:

- Creating accurate and concise delivery timetables.

- Monitoring multiple projects.

- Keeping a close check on the arrival of shipments.

- Managing teams and staff.

- Ensuring team performance and targets are met.

Job Requirements

You must have a degree in science, or engineering. Ideally, you will be able to show that you have demonstrated leadership in the past, and taken charge of work-based teams.

Skillset

- You must be a great team worker.

- You must be a good communicator.

- You must be organised.

- You must be a good leader.

Contracts Engineer

 Contracts engineers are enormously important. Essentially, when a drilling company wants work, they take contracts from relevant organisations. It is the job of the contract engineer to decipher which of these contracts is the most suitable. Contracts engineers also play an important role in estimating project costs, keeping costs under control, and ensuring the company has a full and detailed appreciation of the scope of the job, and the risks involved. As a contract engineer, your responsibilities will include:

- Conducting negotiations with contractors, and reviewing bids for the company's services.

- Ensuring that every contractual obligation the company enters into, will serve the best interests of the company.

- Reviewing documentation.

- Building a rapport with suppliers, with the intention of securing future commercial work for the company.

- Monitoring company finances and projected expenditure, on a project-basis.

Job Requirements

Given the importance of this role, most companies will expect you to have at least a degree, in quantity surveying, engineering, or law. Business degrees will also be looked upon favourably. Professional qualifications in surveying or procurement will really help your cause.

Skillset

- You must have fantastic communication skills, not just spoken but verbal too.

- You must be an analytical person.

- You must have excellent attention to detail.

- You must be good with numbers.

Crane Operator

While it might not seem the most glamourous of positions, crane operators play a very important role in both offshore and onshore operations. There's an enormous amount of equipment to be moved, all in an efficient, cost-effective and safe manner, and this is the role of a crane operator. As a crane operator, you will usually work offshore, but there are also positions available in shipyards and other naval bases. As a crane operator, your duties will include:

- Operating cranes, in a safe and competent manner, in accordance with the instructions of platform management.

- Ensuring that crane work is done in a way that adheres to safety protocols, and manufacturing instructions.

- Carrying out routine checks on crane related equipment, to ensure there are no faults or safety hazards.

Job Requirements

The majority of companies will ask for you to demonstrate some experience in marine operations, and that you can show a working understanding of lifting operation protocol and procedures. In terms of qualifications, you will normally be expected to be stage 2 crane operator qualified.

Skillset

- You must be a responsible person, who can work in adherence to health and safety protocols.

- You must be a good communicator.

- You must be able to work as part of a team.

Diver

 Divers are an essential element of the offshore team, and perform a variety of crucial tasks. Since the gas and oil supplies are deep under the surface, offshore companies need divers to carry out essential tasks deep underwater, such as welding. Working as an offshore diver is extremely difficult. You'll be subject to harsh ocean conditions, impacted by the weather. As an offshore diver, your tasks will include:

- Carrying out essential maintenance work, such as non-destructive testing and inspection of the extraction site.

- Communicating with the engineering team, to inform them about the condition of the structure or equipment.

- Assisting with undersea repair work.

- Carrying out maintenance work on deck.

Job Requirements

Given the complexity of this role, there are a variety of things you'll need before you can be accepted. This will include gaining several SCUBA qualifications, a Subsea Inspection and Tooling Certificate, and first aid training. Along with this, most companies will look for divers who have previous professional experience of diving commercially, a BTEC in engineering or similar, and experience in operations such as welding.

Skillset

- You must be adept at risk assessment.

- You must be a great communicator.

- You must be a responsible and safe person.

- You must be resilient and willing to overcome hardships.

Drilling Engineer

 With drilling being such an important element of offshore work, it makes sense that companies would hire drilling engineers. Drilling engineers play an essential role in drilling operations and in the overall lifecycle of a well. They are involved in every single aspect of drilling operations, from assessing the costs of various drilling activities to coordinating the performance of drillers. As a drilling engineer, your tasks will include:

- Planning and overseeing the successful execution of drilling programmes.

- Playing a lead role in designing the well.

- Analysing the performance of the drilling team and establishing how performance and efficiency can be improved.

- Monitoring drilling costs.

Drilling workers can generally be separated into two different categories: derrickman and driller.

Derrickman/Derrickhand. When working as a derrickman, your job is to deal with common issues related to the derrick – which is the name for the mast that supports the installation drilling equipment. Although the role of a derrickman can vary between drilling rigs, they commonly report to drillers, who supervise said tasks.

As a derrickman, your tasks will include:

- Ensuring the derrick is in good and stable condition.

- Stacking sections of drill pipe.

- Operating lifts and machinery.

- Controlling pumps and pump-related operations.

Driller. Drillers are tasked with supervising the drilling team, and their main role is to ensure that the rate of drilling is consistent and correct. Drillers ensure that all operations on the drill floor are completed using the correct safety operations, and that maintenance is performed on crucial equipment. The driller is responsible for ensuring that the well is drilled to the correct parameters, as decided by the operator.

As a driller, your tasks will include:

- Taking leadership of drill floor operations.

- Controlling the machinery on the drill floor.

- Keeping and maintaining accurate records of the day's drilling.

- Ensuring every person on the team follows the correct health and safety protocols.

Job Requirements

In order to work as a drilling engineer, you will need to have degree in either science or engineering. Employers will assess you against your communication, leadership, and teamwork skills.

Skillset

- You must be a great communicator.

- You must have fantastic teamwork skills.

- You must be a good motivator and organiser.

- You must be analytical and able to problem solve.

Electrical Engineer

With such an enormous amount of technology being used onboard offshore facilities, it's imperative that there are electrical engineers on hand to fix problems, and monitor performance. As an electrical engineer, you aren't just there to solve issues, you will also be expected to design and develop the systems onboard, to increase efficiency. A huge focus of your role is on safety, and ensuring that the technology onboard the facility is running reliably. As an electrical engineer, you will need to perform tasks such as:

- Providing offshore employees with technical support and assistance.

- Monitoring electrical/equipment performance, to ensure offshore operations are running efficiently.

- Ensuring that all electrical equipment onboard a facility meets with health and safety requirements.

- Analysing electrical problems, and finding solutions.

- Playing a lead role in the electrical budgeting process.

Job Requirements

Generally, companies will expect you to have a HND in an engineering related subject, and a degree.

Skillset

- You must be an excellent communicator.

- You must be safety conscious.

- You must be a good team worker.

- You must be flexible and adaptable.

- You must be able to find creative solutions to problems.

Environmental Advisor

Environmental advisors play a crucial role in ensuring that companies meet with environmental standards, and that they consider the impact of operations on an environmental scale. Usually, environmental advisors are there to provide important support and advice, as to how said companies can complete tasks in a way which does not harm the environment. As an environmental advisor, your tasks will include:

- Performing environmental assessments of the area in which work will be taking place.

- Visiting offshore sites and assessing the impact that potential work would have on the environment.

- Coordinating with platform management, to maintain records of work that is being done.

- Ensuring that offshore rigs are complying with environmental standards.

- In the event of incidents, you will be asked to carry out environmental investigations, and then produce reports based on these.

Job Requirements

You will likely need a degree in an area related to environmental care/wellbeing. A postgraduate degree is also highly welcomed.

Skillset

- You will need to be a good communicator.

- You will need to be an organised person, who can perform accurate risk assessment.

- You must be able to identify problems and present solutions to these.

- You must be willing to travel between locations, spending time away from home.

Health and Safety Officer

Given the importance of health and safety in offshore work, it's no surprise that many offshore platforms will hire designated health and safety officers. These persons essentially take an advisory role, providing guidance to the company on how accidents can be prevented whilst offshore. As a health and safety officer, your duties will include:

- Working with company management, to develop health and safety policies.

- Conduct inspections of the rig, performing risk assessments and establishing where improvements can be made.

- Provide advice and guidance on health and safety.

- Help staff with critical areas such as protective clothing or safety drills.

- Take part in investigations, in the event of an accident or incident.

Job Requirements

Ordinarily, you will need to demonstrate that you have an NEBOSH certificate – National Examinations Board in Occupational Safety and Health, or a National General Certificate in Occupational Health and Safety.

Skillset

- You must have great communication skills, clearly explaining your ideas.

- You must be able to work with others, in a friendly and amiable manner.

- You must be able to take leadership of situations, and teach others.

- You must be able to perform accurate risk assessments, efficiently identifying potential problems.

Helicopter Pilot

Helicopter pilots are an important part of offshore life, transporting employees from land to sea. Usually there are two pilots per helicopter – captain and co-pilot. As an offshore helicopter pilot, your tasks will include:

- Conducting flight plans, to ensure safe passage.

- Checking weather conditions and airspace rules and regulations prior to flying.

- Ensuring all helicopter equipment is in full working order/ conducting safety checks of the helicopter prior to take-off.

- Using skills and expertise to navigate the helicopter from A to B.

- Filling in post-flight reports, following each journey.

Job Requirements

The majority of employers will ask for candidates to have a private pilot's license, a significant number of hours total flying time, and a commercial pilot's license. You may also be required to have an airline transport pilot's license.

Skillset

- You must have fantastic attention to detail.

- You must have excellent communication skills.

- You must be able to adapt to difficult situations.

- You must be flexible.

- You must be prepared to work long hours.

Helideck Assistant

 Helideck Assistants are tasked with assisting helicopter operations – focusing mainly on ensuring the safe landing and departure of flights, carrying offshore personal from A to B. Naturally, it's essential that helicopter transport is conducted in a safe manner, ensuring the wellbeing of every person on the aircraft. As a Helideck assistant, your tasks will include:

- Assisting with platform preparations, including marking escape routes and assisting with safety plans.
- Playing a key role in the safe landing of offshore Helicopters.
- Working as part of the Emergency Response Team.
- Carrying out maintenance on offshore equipment.
- Refuelling helicopters.
- Fulfilling Banksman-slinger duties, such as rigging and slinging.

Job Requirements

You will need to be Helideck Assistant certified, to an OPITO standard. Most employers will have expected you to complete basic offshore emergency training. Many employers will also ask for you to have an offshore emergency helideck team member certificate, and a helicopter refuelling certificate.

Skillset

- You must have fantastic attention to detail.
- You must have excellent communication skills.
- You must be able to adapt to difficult situations.
- You must be flexible.
- You must be prepared to work long hours.

Instrument Engineer

The role of an instrument engineer is to operate the measuring instruments onboard an offshore rig. These instruments are fundamental to the running of the automated systems that keep things ticking over. Usually, an instrument engineer is responsible for ensuring said systems are running reliably, productively and in a stable fashion. Other tasks include:

-   Providing technical support to offshore employees.

-   Monitoring electrical instruments and systems, to ensure they meet the correct standards.

-   Ensuring that measuring equipment meets the relevant health and safety requirements.

-   Creating regular performance logs on the efficiency of offshore systems.

-   Assisting management with inspection and testing of equipment.

Job Requirements

Usually you will need at least a degree in an engineering related field, and some employers will ask for you to have a HND too, along with evidence of work experience.

Skillset

-   You must be an excellent communicator.

-   You must be safety conscious.

-   You must be a good team worker.

-   You must be flexible and adaptable.

-   You must be able to find creative solutions to problems.

Logistics Controller

The role of a logistics controller is to arrange the transport of equipment from onshore locations to offshore locations. Obviously, this is hugely important, and therefore offshore companies have a dedicated role simply for organising all of this. It's absolutely vital that the right equipment is in the right place, in time, lest the company risk both money and the safety of staff. As a logistics controller, your tasks will include:

- Preparing shipments for transportation to offshore locations.

- Maintaining essential documentation/completing accurate paperwork.

- Obtaining particular specification for certain, more dangerous items, prior to transportation.

- Dealing with transport costs.

- Organising insurance for transported goods.

- Keeping an organised delivery schedule, and ensuring essential persons are kept informed of delivery times and dates.

Job Requirements

The majority of employers will look for candidates who have previous experience working in a logistics-based field. Ideally, you will have experience in dealing with the transportation of hazardous goods.

Skillset

- You must be a highly organised person, capable of multi-tasking.

- You must be a fantastic communicator.

- You must be capable of leading others.

- You must be flexible and calm under pressure.

Maintenance Supervisor

Maintenance supervisors are there to supervise offshore maintenance, not just in oil and gas, but with the systems onboard the platform too. Maintenance supervisors will generally report to the Offshore Installation Manager, whilst working directly with offshore supervisors and staff onshore too. As a maintenance supervisor, your tasks will include:

- Managing the overall process of performing maintenance work.

- Directing and controlling a team of technicians.

- Ensuring that maintenance work is done to the correct health and safety standards.

- Coordinating with managers, to implement essential maintenance work.

- Communicating with engineers onshore.

Job Requirements

Most employers will be looking for candidates who have experience working as an offshore technician, or as a maintenance engineer.

Skillset

- You must be a fantastic communicator.

- You must be capable of leading teams and managing others.

- You must be organised.

- You must be analytical.

Marine Engineer

This is a highly specialised role. Marine engineers are responsible for designing, testing, building and repairing marine vessels. They also provide the design for offshore rigs and equipment, and oversee the building of facilities. Marine Engineers are incredibly valuable to the oil and gas industry, as they provide companies with essential knowledge and expertise, which ensures that the highest possible standards are met. As a marine engineer, your tasks will include:

- Designing offshore rigs and equipment.

- Playing an essential role in the construction of offshore rigs.

- Performing essential maintenance work on offshore installations and vessels.

- Managing repairs on systems and machinery.

- Liaising with the contractor in regards to project timelines, and helping to ensure that projects are completed on time.

Job Requirements

You will need a BTEC, HNC or HND, or a degree in an engineering related subject. Any previous training as an engineering officer in the armed forces will be very useful.

Skillset

- You must be an organised and highly disciplined person.

- You must be a great team player, capable of working with others.

- You must be efficient, flexible and adaptable.

- You must be a fantastic problem solver.

Mechanical Technician

Mechanical technicians are responsible for conducting both planned and unplanned maintenance tasks, as well as repair tasks, on offshore equipment, such as pumps or turbines. Naturally, this is a very important role. Essential maintenance contributes massively to safe working practices onboard offshore facilities. As a mechanical technician, your tasks will include:

- Testing equipment, and carrying out essential maintenance.

- Conducting fault-finding assessments on offshore systems and equipment.

- Modifying and repairing equipment.

- Playing a leading role in offshore facility risk assessments.

- Creating maintenance and safety reports, on a regular basis.

Job Requirements

The majority of employers will require you to have a recognised trade apprenticeship, or an NVQ Level 3 in a relevant subject. It is also useful if you can demonstrate that you've taken part in the OPITO Technician training scheme.

Skillset

- You must be an excellent communicator.

- You must be safety conscious.

- You must be a good team worker.

- You must be flexible and adaptable.

- You must be able to find creative solutions to problems.

Mudlogger

Mudlogger is a research-based position. Mudloggers monitor the information that comes in from drilling operations, analyse this, and then help the drilling team to use this information in further operations. In order to do this, they collect rock samples. The analysis conducted by mudloggers is extremely important to the overall production process. As a mudlogger, your responsibilities will include:

-   Collecting, processing and analysing samples of rock.

-   Using computer analysis to interpret information, and help the drilling team to use this.

-   Monitoring drilling operations using computer software.

-   Creating written reports, with the aim of assisting future operations.

Job Requirements

The majority of employers will look for mudloggers to have a HND in a related subject, and ideally prospective candidates will have both a degree and evidence of work experience.

Skillset

-   You must have fantastic attention to detail.

-   You must have excellent communication skills.

-   You must be flexible.

-   You must be an analytical person, who can problem solve.

-   You must be able to analyse complex statistics and data/ information.

Pipefitter

Pipefitters are responsible for fitting pipework to offshore facilities, to meet the requirements of well operations. As a pipefitter, you can work either onshore or offshore, usually in shifts. Your typical tasks will include:

-    Using engineering diagrams as a basis for your work.

-    Cross checking numbers and calculations, prior to assembly.

-    Fabricating pipework to the allocated standards.

-    Cutting pipes to the correct size/specification, using the correct equipment.

-    Grinding casings, so that they can be welded.

Job Requirements

In order to become a pipefitter, you will generally need demonstrable welding or grinding experience, and a trades certification. Certain apprenticeships are very helpful, and it's good if you have experience in particular types of pipework.

Skillset

-    You must be an organised and highly disciplined person.

-    You must be a great team player, capable of working with others.

-    You must be efficient, flexible and adaptable.

-    You must be a fantastic problem solver.

Plater

Plating is a very important duty onboard offshore installations. Platers are responsible for ensuring that structures and pipe work are installed to the appropriate standards and guidelines. This is also a viable role onshore. Typical duties of a plater include:

- Using specification diagrams to ensure the right shape and cut, and also using specialised equipment, such as flame-cutting machines.

- Cutting steel.

- Using techniques such as drilling and sawing.

- Ensuring that all work is conducted in line with health and safety standards and procedures.

Job Requirements

Most employers will look for you to have a relevant trade apprenticeship, along with basic offshore induction and emergency training. Any demonstrable experience in manual labour will be welcomed.

Skillset

- You must be an organised and highly disciplined person.

- You must be a great team player, capable of working with others.

- You must be efficient, flexible and adaptable.

- You must be a fantastic problem solver.

Reservoir Engineer

Reservoir engineers work with technical divisions to extract oil and gas. In order to do this, they turn geological information into models, which aim to predict the way in which oil, gas and water flow through rocks. As such, there's a lot of prediction, simulation and analysis in this field. As a reservoir engineer, your typical tasks will include:

- Providing accurate forecasts of the way in which oil and gas flow.

- Ensuring extraction plans are economical and viable.

- Helping to locate the right places for wells.

- Estimating the scale of oil and gas reserves.

- Analysing technical data.

Job Requirements

Having a degree in an engineering related subject is generally a prerequisite to this career. Any further qualifications, such as a Masters, are much appreciated.

Skillset

- You must be a great communicator.

- You must have fantastic teamwork skills.

- You must be a good motivator and organiser.

- You must be analytical and able to problem solve.

ROV (Remotely Operated Vehicle) Technician

An ROV technician is responsible for operating and maintaining the ROV tools and equipment, which are essential for offshore projects. ROV equipment can vary, depending on your speciality. Obviously, it's essential that the person operating the ROV equipment has an expert understanding of what they are doing, and that they can work to the correct health and safety standards. As an ROV technician, your tasks will include:

- Operating and working with ROV systems, under the supervision of the superintendent.

- Helping to assemble and evaluate new ROV systems and equipment.

- Completing post-job reports, using skills like fault finding and evaluative techniques to establish where things went well, and what could be improved.

- Administering maintenance to ROV systems and equipment.

- Working with other departments on board the vessel, to ensure projects run smoothly.

Job Requirements

Most employers will ask for you to have at least a BTEC in an engineering related field. Any understanding and practical experience of the systems that you'll be working with go a long way to securing the job.

Skillset

- You must have fantastic attention to detail.

- You must have excellent communication skills.

- You must be flexible.

- You must be an analytical person, who can problem solve.

- You must be able to analyse complex statistics and data/ information.

Subsea Engineer

Subsea Engineers are tasked with designing and then installing subsea structures and equipment, such as wellheads and pipelines. There are a wide variety of companies who hire subsea engineers, including operators and engineering consultant companies. As a subsea engineer, your tasks could include:

- Offering technical support to offshore or onshore teams.

- Helping with the wellhead installation, and the installation of pipelines.

- Creating budgets and plans for specific projects, and playing a key role in the financial management process.

- Clearly communicating with colleagues and site workers.

Job Requirements

Ideally, you will have a HDN in a related subject, and demonstrable work experience. Companies will usually look for candidates who are ready and willing to become chartered engineers.

Skillset

- You must be an excellent communicator.

- You must be able to work as part of a team.

- You must be able to demonstrate leadership skills.

- You must be an analytical person, who can problem solve.

Welder

 A welder is someone who cuts and then joins metals and other materials together, using special techniques. This is extremely important on an offshore rig, and welders are needed for an enormous variety of tasks – even in constructing the rig itself. As a welder, your tasks will include:

- Selecting the correct materials for various tasks.

- Following complex engineering diagrams, to product the best possible results.

- Deciding on the right welding methods for specific tasks.

- Inspecting and assessing the quality of cutting and welding work.

- Adhering to health and safety standards.

Job Requirements

Usually you will need a welding qualification. Upon application, it's likely that that the employer will ask you to take a specific test, to demonstrate that you can perform the type of welding work required for the job.

Skillset

- You must be an organised and highly disciplined person.

- You must be a great team player, capable of working with others.

- You must be efficient, flexible and adaptable.

- You must be a fantastic problem solver.

Well Test Engineer

Well Test Engineers play a crucial role in well test operations, including planning projects, assessing equipment, and managing personnel. Usually, well test engineers are hired by drilling companies or specialist well service companies, which then contract them out to the offshore operators. As a well test engineer, your tasks could include:

-    Playing a key part in the support of well operations, on a daily basis.

-    Helping to plan projects, ensuring that they are in line with safety standards.

-    Collecting data and presenting this in a succinct and organised fashion to clients.

-    Working with the Operations Supervisor, to provide technical support.

Job Requirements

Usually you will need at least a BTEC in engineering. Most employers will look for candidates who have a degree in an engineering related field, and who already have experience and knowledge of offshore projects and work.

Skillset

-    You must be a great communicator.

-    You must have fantastic teamwork skills.

-    You must be a good motivator and organiser.

-    You must be analytical and able to problem solve.

Routes Into Offshore Work

So, now we've looked at the various career options available, let's take a look at some potential routes into offshore work.

Apprenticeships

The majority of companies offer entry-level apprenticeships to aspiring offshore workers. Again, the requirements for these apprenticeships will vary, but the majority of employers will ask you to be over the age of 18, and have 4 GCSEs – usually English, Maths, Science, or Design and Technology. Although you will start off as a roustabout (which we'll cover in great detail later on), there are numerous opportunities for progression, and the company will train you to improve your skills.

As an apprentice, your primary tasks will include keeping things clean and tidy, securing the deck area, loading equipment, and even painting. You'll be trained to mix drilling mud, and help keep specialised equipment maintained and in good working condition. Whilst doing all of this, you will be trained on other tasks: such as using cranes and specialised lifting equipment (banksman slinger training) and also will be given extensive safety training, in areas such as firefighting and first aid.

Apprentices generally work the same schedule as other employees – that is to say that you will be working onboard the rig for two/three weeks at a time, before spending approximately the same amount of time onshore.

Benefits

The current minimum wage for UK apprentices (as of 2018) is £3.70 per hour. However, given the nature of the role, it's likely that you'll be earning a bit more than this. As an apprentice, the company will want to train you so that you can become an extremely valuable asset – and this means that you will pick up a huge variety of skills whilst doing so. Furthermore, even though you are still an apprentice, you are entitled to the same employment rights and benefit rights as any other person. As an apprentice, you'll likely develop a closer relationship with your employer than you would otherwise, as they'll be closely monitoring your progress and improvement.

Once you've completed your apprenticeship, you aren't guaranteed to be offered a job, but if you have performed well then it's highly likely! Lots of employers actually prefer to take on apprentices, as there's less risk to this than hiring employees. They get to see your work ethic and ability before they take you on full time, instead of just hiring you right off the bat.

Of course, you can also take an apprenticeship in many of the jobs we've listed, if you've already got some experience and skills.

How To Apply

Applying for apprenticeships shouldn't be too difficult, although you can expect fairly tough competition. A quick internet search should bring up a variety of companies who are looking to hire offshore apprentices. You may be expected to complete an application form, and a quick psychometric test. Later in this book, we'll provide you with in-depth tips on how to pass the tests.

Graduate Schemes

The majority of offshore companies will offer some kind of graduate scheme. These graduate schemes provide candidates with hands on experience, and aim to elevate them into management positions.

The type of graduate scheme that you are on will largely depend upon the company that you are applying for. However, here's an example of how your graduate scheme might be structured:

Year One

During the first year of a graduate scheme, candidates will undertake two placements, rotating between different departments. The majority of graduates will be placed in management-based fields, such as operational support, accounts, or sales. Essentially, the aim is to give candidates a full experience of the industry, and help them to understand the offshore business. In year one, they'll gain a beginner's insight into how offshore projects are run, and the fundamentals of areas such as proposals, project planning and customer service.

Year Two

Year two is generally very similar to year one. Again, candidates will take two placements, for 6 months each. Now, however, candidates will be expected to play a more detailed role in aspects like project planning and business management, and will need to use the lessons they learned during the first year in accordance with this.

Year Three

In year three, you will be asked to select a specialism. By this point, you'll have spent two years working within the industry, so you should have a good idea of which field interests you the most. Following this, you will spend the final year of the graduate scheme working within this role. You'll be given the chance to obtain professional qualifications in the specialism, or to complete a post-graduate study in the subject.

Common fields chosen include:

- Sales.

- Project Management.

- Hydrographics.

- Health and Safety.

- Quality Management.

- Electrical Superintendence.

Benefits

By far the biggest benefit of graduate schemes is that they give you a leg-up in the industry, providing you with the chance to work in positions which would normally be very hard to obtain. You'll learn on the job, with the help of mentors and experienced line managers, leaning from their experience and knowledge. Not only that, but you will learn which field you are most suited for, whilst gaining a wider knowledge of the industry as a whole as you go.

How to Apply for Graduate Schemes

The majority of companies, if they do offer a graduate scheme, will ask for candidates who have a relevant degree. For example, it would be useful to have a degree in a subject such as business management or finance. You'll have to go through a pretty tough selection process too – from submitting a CV to online tests, and then a competency-based interview. In this book, we'll cover all of these elements.

Becoming a Roustabout

In this section, we'll provide you with an in-depth insight into applying for a position as a roustabout. This section will include top tips on the application form, and the interview process. However, please note that the tips within this section will not just be relevant for roustabouts, but for other jobs too. Our CV, application and interview advice can be applied to any offshore position - learn the competencies and you will be successful!

Roustabout is the most general, entry-level position on a rig. Roustabouts are generally expected to perform basic tasks, which are essential for keeping the installation in working order. This includes tasks such as:

- Keeping the drilling area clean and tidy.

- Offloading supplies.

- Stacking equipment.

- Repairing equipment.

- Assisting other crew members with tasks.

- Helping crane operators.

- Loading boats.

Roustabouts play a really important role on offshore rigs, and things wouldn't be able to function without them. However, working as a roustabout is seriously demanding. Physically, you will be pushed to the limits, and you'll need to work in a variety of weather conditions, plus you must be able to deal with heights.

Qualifications

Becoming an offshore roustabout is actually quite simple, and you don't need any specific qualifications in order to get a job. It's quite common for people to become an apprentice first. If you are taking an apprenticeship scheme, then usually employers will ask for you to have four GCSEs, from A* grade to C, with Maths, English, Science or Technology being preferred.

Although you don't need formal qualifications to gain a job as a roustabout, any experience will help. For example, if you've worked in areas such as shipbuilding, or construction, then this will greatly aid your chances of gaining the position – or any other related fields. Furthermore, in order to work in any position offshore, you'll need to pass a variety of safety tests. This includes: an offshore survival course, a firefighting course, emergency response training, and an induction. You also need to be 18 years old to work as a roustabout.

Behavioural Requirements

As with any offshore job, there are certain behavioural requirements that roustabouts must adhere to. Offshore workers are unable to drink alcohol, take drugs, or smoke whilst on the rig. You must be prepared for the physical demands of this role. Roustabouts work in hazardous conditions, and are often asked to handle hazardous materials too. To protect themselves, roustabouts are required to wear protective clothing whilst on duty, and this will often include a safety harness.

As a roustabout, it's imperative that you are able to work as a member of a team, and that you have the practical skills to manage tasks whilst offshore. The latter might sound simple enough, but not everyone is practically inclined. In order to get you up to speed with things, your employer will put through you a sustained period of training. Ideally, the aim is for roustabouts to increase their competency level, and advance to a higher position on the rig – such as becoming a vehicle operator. Training is available to roustabouts, enabling them to progress to more skill-based positions, such as derrickman or driller.

Core Competencies

As with any job, in any industry, roustabouts (and other offshore workers) must adhere to a set of job-specific core competencies. Core competencies are essentially a set of behavioural guidelines for employees to follow. They outline the expectations of the company, and also form a very important part of the application process. This is even more essential when working on an offshore rig, where correct safety procedures are absolutely integral. When you go through the application process, you'll be expected to demonstrate these competencies throughout.

Applying For Jobs

Most of the time, your application for a roustabout role will be done online. A quick google search should bring you up a variety of positions to apply for, whether you are a specialist looking to join the drill or engineering team, or a roustabout looking for a starting point. Below we've provided you with a sample application form. For the purposes of this book, we've used a job application for a roustabout as a basic example. The tips contained in this section will be useful for any person looking to join an offshore rig.

Sample Job Application

Job Position: Roustabout

Wage: £19,000 per year.

Start date: Two-weeks induction, starting 09/10/18, followed by immediate transferal to offshore facility.

Company Ethos and Philosophy
Derick Matthews Drilling is a national leader in deepwater drilling. We are a highly respected company, looking to employ a number of roustabouts for an offshore facility – located in the North Sea. As a company, we carry out contracted drilling work, with the aim of solving national deepwater issues. Derick Matthews Drilling plays a leading role in sustaining the environment, and protecting the natural world.

Roustabouts play an essential role on our facilities, and we are dedicated to providing all staff with as much training as possible, to ensure that they are as skilled as possible.

Roustabouts will work on a three-week shift pattern, followed by two-weeks on shore, and so forth. Derick Matthews Drilling will provide entry-level roustabouts with BOSIET training, during an induction period.

Key Responsibilities:

As a roustabout onboard our facility, your primary responsibilities will be as follows:

- Acting as a crucial member of the roustabout crew, and reporting to your Team Leader.

- Adhering to the company health, safety and quality policies, and helping your colleagues to do the same. Derick Matthews drilling staff members must adhere to the company's environmental policy, at all times.

- Monitoring hazards whilst onboard the facility and reporting these to the relevant persons – your team leader or other senior staff.

- Assisting mechanics and engineers with machine maintenance, such as carrying out daily checks on drilling equipment and cranes.

- Ensuring that all work is performed to the standards laid out by the Derick Matthews training manual, and via our established quality assurance system – Derick Matthews Quality Assurance (D.M.Q.A).

- Working with your colleagues to provide a safe working environment for specialist drillers, and performing routine tasks, such as pulling, lifting, and carrying.

- Participating in safety-training and quality assurance exercises, on a weekly basis.

Other Responsibilities include:
- Communicating effectively and efficiently with other crew members and team leaders.

- Working in a way which shows the highest possible regard for the safety of everyone onboard the facility.

- Assisting with tasks such as anchor handling, and deck work, including carrying out construction and repair operations, inventory preparation, safety assessment, and protective coat maintenance.

Derick Matthews drilling roustabouts are expected to act as a key part of the facility emergency response team, and therefore you can expect sustained training if successful.

Qualifications

In order to be valid for selection, you must adhere to the following:

- You must have legal rights to work within Britain/The United Kingdom, without any restrictions.

- You must be comfortable working away from home for periods of 18 days or more.

- You must be able to show a valid UK passport.

- You must be able to show evidence of MIST certification.

- You must be able to provide evidence that you have passed an OGUK Offshore Medical within the past two years.

Candidates will need to complete an online application form, pass a telephone interview, and then attend an interview at our HQ – in London. There will also be an online situational judgement test.

How To Look At This

Okay, so, now you've looked at a sample job application form, you need to establish how this can be broken down. Obviously, there's quite a huge amount of information here which needs to be considered, so it's important that you can break down this information and separate out the most important bits. Once you do this, you start to hone in on what matters most to the employer, and start using this information in your job application answers and interview.

Let's start by looking at the company ethos and philosophy:

Derick Matthews drilling is a <u>national leader</u> in deepwater drilling. <u>We are a highly respected company</u>, looking to employ a number of roustabouts for an offshore facility – located in the North Sea. As a company, we carry out contracted drilling work, with <u>the aim of solving national deepwater issues</u>. <u>Derick Matthews drilling plays a leading role in sustaining the environment, and protecting the natural world</u>. Roustabouts play an essential role on our facilities, and <u>we are dedicated to providing all staff with as much training as possible, to ensure that they are as skilled as possible</u>.

Roustabouts will work on a three-week shift pattern, followed by two-weeks on shore, and so forth. Derick Matthews Drilling will provide entry-level roustabouts with BOSIET training, during an induction period.

As you can see, above we've highlighted certain parts. These parts all contain essential information, which can be used later in the process. Here's how:

'National leader' 'Highly respected company' – When you are responding to application form and interview questions, you should definitely make reference to the company's reputation.

'With the aim of solving national deepwater issues' 'Sustaining the environmental and protecting the natural world' – This is another essential piece of information, and can be used in the interview and application form responses. Obviously you should always be truthful with your employer, but if you really care and are passionate about the environment then this is a great way to link your own moral values with theirs. Companies want to employ people who are passionate about the same things as them, and who share their moral standards and values.

'We are dedicated to providing all staff with as much training as possible, to ensure that they are as skilled as possible.' – This shows that the company are looking for employees who are willing to train and improve their skills whilst working on the offshore facility.

Therefore, this is a quality about yourself that you should really try and push.

Now, let's look at the key responsibilities. See if you can take the same approach as above, and then have a look at our list to compare:

'Acting as a crucial member of the roustabout crew' – This shows that you need teamwork skills, one of the core competencies.

'Adhering to the company health, safety and quality policies, and helping your colleagues to do the same' – You'll notice that this job description emphasises health and safety on several occasions. As we've already explained, health and safety is absolutely vital when working on an offshore rig, so it's understandable that the company want someone with an appreciation for this.

'Monitoring hazards whilst onboard the facility and reporting these to the relevant persons – your team leader or other senior staff' – This relates to the core competencies of communication and organisation.

'Assisting mechanics and engineers with machine maintenance' – This relates to the core competency of mechanical knowledge.

'Working with your colleagues to provide a safe working environment for specialist drillers, and performing routine tasks, such as pulling, lifting, and carrying' – This relates to the core competencies of physical fitness and discipline.

As you can see, a wide range of competencies have been covered here. All of these are important things to remember when it comes to the application and interview questions. However, there's another way you can use all of this too – in your cover letter and CV.

Now that we've worked out how to break down the application form into behaviours that the employer is looking for, let's incorporate these into a cover letter.

Cover Letter

When applying for a job as a roustabout, the application process will very much depend on the rig that you are applying for. Some rigs will ask that you simply fill in an application form online, whereas others will ask you to send in a CV and Cover letter, and some will ask you to do all three. In this section we will look at how to construct a CV and Cover Letter.

Let's start out with the Cover Letter.

What is a Cover Letter?

In case you aren't familiar with the concept of writing a cover letter, a cover letter is essentially a precursor to your CV. It tells the employer:

- Who you are.

- Why you want to work on this particular rig.

- What your skills and qualities are.

- What you would bring to the company.

Whilst a CV is essentially a structured and organised document, which allows the employer to see your skills and qualifications, a cover letter is a more formal piece of writing that allows you to express yourself a bit better. Think of it like a 'getting to know you', before the employer looks at the all-important CV. You absolutely should use the job description when writing your cover letter. Try and get as many of the behavioural characteristics as you can into your letter, showing the employer that you are someone they should be hiring.

The way to structure your cover letter is as follows:

⇒ Paragraph 1 – Introduce yourself to the employer, and tell them why you want to work for their company.

⇒ Paragraph 2 – Give an overview of your skills and qualities.

⇒ Paragraph 3 – Conclude, by explaining why they should hire you.

When writing your cover letter, you need to ensure that it's grammatically correct, and contains no spelling or punctuation errors. Remember that you are trying to convince the employer about the quality of your work, so leaving sloppy mistakes in your first letter will not help. Make sure you proofread the letter until you are happy with it, or ask a friend to look over it for you. Furthermore, remember that this is a formal letter. You are addressing a prospective employer, so you need to show a level of respect.

Below we've provided you with a sample cover letter for the job description above. Take a look at this, and then try to write your own.

<u>Sample Cover Letter</u>

Dear Sir/Madam,

I am writing to you to apply for the role of roustabout, as per your job description. I am an enthusiastic, hardworking and safety-conscious individual, with a fantastic work ethic. I believe that I'd be really suited for a job on one of your offshore facilities, and that the tasks listed in your job description are the perfect fit for me. Of course, your company is well-known to me, and I would be honoured to work for an organisation as esteemed as Derick Matthews Drilling. Having studied your website and ethos, I was delighted to discover that your company takes such a keen interest and care in environmental matters. This is a matter which is very close to my heart, and therefore was very appealing for me.

Although I do not have any previous experience of working on an offshore rig, I believe that I have a number of qualities and skills which would put me in good stead. I have always had a keen interest in engineering, and with this in mind I have spent a great deal of my spare time working in my father's garage – where I have dealt with the mechanics of vehicles, and resolving mechanically based problems. Furthermore, my current job – working as a warehouse operations officer in Kent, has provided me with training in areas such as health and safety, lifting and manual operations, and machinery operation – including vehicle management.

I believe that my personal ethos, values, and skills, match up extremely well with what you are looking for, and I would be extremely grateful if you would consider me for this position, and I look forward to hearing from you.

Yours Sincerely,

Martin Parrish.

Hopefully the above should give you an idea of how to construct a cover letter, using the job description keywords as a guideline.

Now, let's move onto creating a CV!

Your CV

You are probably familiar with the concept of a CV, and what it represents, but there are lots of professional rules surrounding CVs that many people don't know – and not adhering to these can really set you back when it comes to passing. Furthermore, the way you lay out your CV is really important. A good layout can mean the difference between moving on to the next stage, and failing the application process. This doesn't mean that you need to construct your CV using lots of fancy design elements, simply that it needs to be a tidy, relevant and easy-to-read document, that clearly allows the employer to find the information they need in a short space of time.

There are many different ways to structure your CV, but generally the best approach is this:

- Start out by giving the employer a 2-paragraph personal profile.

- Next, write a paragraph about your skills and qualities.

- Following this, list your education, and then your employment history.

- Finish by writing a short paragraph about your interests and hobbies, and then include some references (if applicable).

Your CV should ideally be no longer than 2 A4 pages in length, and should present things in a way that makes it easy for the employer to find what they are looking for.

Below we've provided you with a template on how to do this:

Sample CV

10 Ficshire Lane, Ficville City
MartinParrish@gmail.com
01234 5678910
Martin Parrish

PERSONAL PROFILE

I am a responsible, hardworking and enthusiastic person, who is experienced in manual handling roles. The idea of working offshore is extremely appealing to me, and even more so in that I would be working for an organisation that is held in such high regard. I am someone who cares deeply about the quality of my work, and with this in mind I take extensive steps to manage my fitness, and stay mentally and physically sharp.

I believe that my experience working in warehouse operations for the past 4 years would greatly help me in this role, and that I would be a fantastic asset to your company.

SKILLS AND QUALITIES

I am extremely organised, and have a wealth of professional experience managing and working in teams. Throughout my career, I have worked in fields such as warehouse operations, packing units and manual labour. Therefore, I fully understand the importance of taking an efficient and organised approach, and my time management is second to none.

I consider myself to be a highly disciplined person, with a fantastic work ethic. In my last position, I achieved a promotion in a very short space of time – and this was down to my quality of work and dedication to the task. As a team leader, all of my subordinates can verify that I am a fantastic motivator, who brings the best out of every single person under my charge.

Last year, in preparation for a job working offshore, I undertook my BOSIET training, and also obtained my Offshore Medical Certificate. I am fully certified for working offshore, and now I would welcome the chance to put my skills to good use.

EDUCATION AND TRAINING

- GCSE English and Mathematics, Grade B. GCSE Science, Grade C.

- Certificate of Basic offshore induction and emergency training.

- Certificate of Offshore Medical Training.

- NVQ Level 3, City and Guilds Forklift Truck Operations

EMPLOYMENT

(April 2013, to date)

Warehouse Manager, Parcels4U

- Working as a Warehouse Manager at Parcels4U, I have delivered above and beyond expectations. I am responsible for the management of the warehouse packing team, on a daily basis, and ensuring that daily, weekly and monthly targets are met. I have helped train staff using essential equipment, such as forklift operation, and also improved the standards of health and safety in the workplace.

- Along with the above, I have also produced and maintained standardised procedures documentation, improved the way in which Parcels4U manage staff absentees and holiday, and also implemented a far better warehouse staff welfare system.

(January 2013 to April 2013)

Warehouse Operative, Parcels4U

- Played a key role in the dispatch of products to customers.

- Operated warehouse machinery, including cranes and forklifts.

- Assisted management in creating a detailed work-schedule, with the aim of improving efficiency.

(October 2010 to December 2012)

Roofing Labourer/General Work, ConstructionCRS

- Assisted senior roofer with tasks such as tiling, stripping, and repairing.

- Assisted with the transportation of building materials, such as timber, and slate.

- Operated essential construction machinery, such as diggers and cranes.

Further work history within the sector available upon request.

INTERESTS AND HOBBIES

When not working, I enjoy keeping myself fit and healthy. I stay active by running 3 times a week, and also play for a local football team.

Application Form

Usually, you'll be asked to send in your CV and Cover Letter along with an online application form. You can find the application form on most company websites. The application form, and filling it in correctly, is extremely important. Not only do you need to be completely truthful with the assessor, but you also need to fill in the all-important competency questions in the right way.

A typical application form will be structured in a way to find out as much information about you as possible. You'll be asked a series of personal questions: name, age, national insurance number, address, etc. and may also be asked to fill in some details on your education and training. Finally, you'll reach the last section – the competency-focused questions.

Not every single employer will use competency-focused questions in the application form, and some may include different types of question. Later in our book, we've provided you with a breakdown of how to answer competency-based questions, but the application form questions will likely be slightly different. Normally, these questions will focus ON the competencies and your understanding of them, rather than when you've demonstrated.

When answering these questions, try to focus on keywords. By this, we mean that you should try to use keywords from the relevant competencies in your response. So, if a question asks you about the importance of problem solving, try and use terms like 'analytical' 'accurate' 'efficient' or 'logical'.

Remember too that for most questions, you will have a word limit. Normally, the form will ask you to answer in 150-200 words or less. If this happens, DO NOT go over the word limit, as you will be penalised. This will show that you are unable to follow simple instructions, which is the last thing you want at this early stage!

Below we've included three examples of these, so that you can see what we mean. We've also provided you with 3 sample responses to these, using the core competencies as a guideline.

Q1. In 200 words or less, tell us about what the term 'health and safety' means to you.

As we've explained, health and safety onboard an offshore rig is absolutely paramount, because there are a huge amount of things which can go wrong. There are so many individual facets to offshore work, and so many safety hazards, that it's essential for everyone to be working in adherence with health and safety standards. In your answer, you need to elaborate on how health and safety protocols protect the people onboard, and why it's important.

Below we've provided you with a sample response to this:

Health and safety means ensuring that every single person onboard the facility has a correct and proper understanding of protocols, and that they are adhering to these at every step of the project. Health and safety protects the welfare of those aboard the vessel, it means that we can work in a responsible and efficient fashion, without physical harm occurring to those working on the facility or off it. I understand that working onboard an offshore rig comes with a large number of hazards, and that there are risks.

As a former warehouse operative, I am fully trained in health and safety and understand the dangers that manual work can present. During every step of the working process, I endeavour to create an environment which is free from hazard and danger to those around me. I understand that I am responsible for the welfare of my colleagues, just as they are for me.

Q2. In 200 words or less, explain to us why teamwork is so important.

Your teamwork and communication skills will form a fundamental part of life onboard an offshore rig. So, it's important for the assessors to establish that you understand why teamwork is important, and that you are a team player. As we've already explained in the competencies, working as part of a cohesive team means that tasks can be performed more efficiently, and to a safe and better standard. So, explain this to the assessor.

Below we've provided you with a sample response to this:

Teamwork is essential, not just in this field, but in the majority of others too. I understand that when working on an offshore rig, I will need to rely on my colleagues just as they will rely on me. Through my research, I have learned that offshore work is certainly not a one-man job, and that it will be the efforts of the team which ultimately determine whether the project has been completed successfully or not.

In terms of health and safety, I believe that a group effort can yield far more productive and reassuring results than any individual effort can. As the saying goes, 'two heads are better than one' and good communication between teammates is essential if we want to succeed.

During my career, I have worked in a variety of different teams, and this has given me a strong level of appreciation for the scale of what a group can achieve, compared to just one person.

Q3. Your organisation skills will be essential when working offshore. In 200 words or less, explain why this is.

As we explained previously, organisation will have a huge impact on your ability to do the job successfully. Given you will be completing multiple tasks, you need to exercise good time management and be able to prioritise tasks. Timing is everything on an offshore rig. Even the slightest delay can significantly impact the project, hurting the reputation and profits of the company as a result. The more organised you are, the better work you can produce, because you'll know how and when things need to be finished, and what's coming next.

Below we've provided you with a sample response to this:

I fully understand that organisation is a vital part of working offshore. As someone who has worked in the warehouse and packing environment, I have a huge amount of experience in working to strict deadlines and being time efficient. I can multi-task, and prioritise different things, both of which I know are very important when working offshore. I understand that deadlines are crucial in offshore work, and that a failure to adhere to the allocated time schedule can lead to a loss of reputation and profits for the company.

Furthermore, I am a highly flexible person. I believe that the more flexible you are, the easier you will find it to organise your tasks – as being flexible means that you are unlikely to be thrown off course by an unexpected task. I am aware that there is a need for a certain degree of flexibility whilst working offshore, where tasks can come up, and will need to take priority over ongoing ones.

Online Aptitude Tests

Following successful completion of the application form, you will be asked to complete some online tests. Given the enormous number of roles available on an offshore rig, it's impossible for us to give you every single test. However, the likelihood is that you will sit two tests: a situational judgement test and a personality test. For some more specialised careers, you might be asked to take a technical assessment.

In this section, we'll provide you with a variety of similar assessments, designed to test your personality, your decision making, and your mechanical awareness.

Please note that the tests in this section are not designed to imitate the actual test that you'll take. They are simply here to help you practice similar types of questions.

The first test that we have prepared for you is a situational judgement test.

Situational Judgement Test

Situational judgement tests are designed to challenge how you would behave in certain scenarios. Your responses to situational judgement questions tell the assessor a great deal about your values, how responsible you are, and your judgement/decision-making skills. Not all situational judgement questions will be focused around offshore work, many of them will put you in real-world scenarios to see how you react.

Usually, for each question you will be given a short passage, describing an incident. This will be followed by 4 statements.

Situational judgement tests can differ in nature. Some tests will ask you to pick just the best answer from the statements, but others will ask you to rank the answers from 1-4, or from 'most efficient' to 'least efficient'.

> You are sitting in the staff canteen, when three other members of the drilling crew sit down at your table. As you engage in friendly discussion with them, two of the members begin to mock the other person for his religion. Although they are only joking, you can see that the individual in question has been upset by these comments.

1. Join in, it's just a bit of banter.

    Efficient | Fairly Efficient | Inefficient | Counterproductive

2. Speak up, and inform your colleagues that they should have more respect for other religions.

    Efficient | Fairly Efficient | Inefficient | Counterproductive

3. Ask the offended colleague to speak to you in private afterwards, where you will discuss the comments.

    Efficient | Fairly Efficient | Inefficient | Counterproductive

4. Try to change the subject.

    Efficient | Fairly Efficient | Inefficient | Counterproductive

How to tackle the question

Whenever you are answering this type of situational judgment question, always try to focus your answer around the 'right thing to do'. You should try to answer truthfully, but you also need to consider about how each answer will make you come across to the assessor.

'Join in, it's just a bit of banter.'

Answer: Counterproductive

Explanation: This is a counterproductive response. Religion is not something that should be mocked, and you can clearly see that the individual in question has taken the remarks badly.

'Speak up, and inform your colleagues that they should have more respect for other religions.'

Answer: Efficient

Explanation: This is an efficient response, as you are clearly demonstrating to the affected individual that discrimination of any kind will not be tolerated, as well as admonishing your colleagues for their behaviour.

'Ask the offended colleague to speak to you in private afterwards, where you will discuss the comments.'

Answer: Fairly Efficient

Explanation: This response is fairly efficient. You are showing your colleague that discrimination is not acceptable, but at the same time you are not demonstrating this to the individuals who have upset him.

'Try to change the subject.'

Answer: Inefficient

Explanation: This is an inefficient response. You need to make sure that the problem is addressed.

Now put your skills to practice with our sample test!

Q1.

> You are working in an office when a member of staff, who is in a wheelchair, approaches you. She asks you if you would be willing to swap desks, as your desk is closer to the exit route, and it will make it easier for her to go to the toilet when required. How do you react?

1. Say no. You are already settled in at your desk and to move would cause unnecessary upheaval.

Efficient | Fairly Efficient | Inefficient | Counterproductive

2. Say yes. This is not a problem for you and you can see why moving desks would help her out and improve her working day.

Efficient | Fairly Efficient | Inefficient | Counterproductive

3. Tell her to speak to your boss first, to see if he is in agreement with her request. If he doesn't have a problem with it, neither do you.

Efficient | Fairly Efficient | Inefficient | Counterproductive

4. Tell her you would be willing to swap desks providing she is prepared to move all of your belongings to the new desk.

Efficient | Fairly Efficient | Inefficient | Counterproductive

Q2.

> You are a train conductor working on your local line. At 10 past 10 in the morning, you are performing your hourly ticket inspection. You come across a man on the train who has not purchased a ticket. He claims that the reason for this is because he had to board the train quickly. It's an emergency as his mother has taken a fall and is in hospital. He has the money to pay the fare there and then. His station is two stops away. What do you do?

1. Consult with the other people in the carriage as to what to do.

   Efficient | Fairly Efficient | Inefficient | Counterproductive

2. Allow him to pay the full ticket fare to his intended stop.

   Efficient | Fairly Efficient | Inefficient | Counterproductive

3. Perform a citizen's arrest. This man is a criminal.

   Efficient | Fairly Efficient | Inefficient | Counterproductive

4. Issue the man with a standard penalty fare.

   Efficient | Fairly Efficient | Inefficient | Counterproductive

Q3.

Your company has recently hired a new staff member. He has only been working for you for 2 days, but you have noticed him making inappropriate remarks towards female staff members. Your manager does not seem to have noticed. One of your female colleagues has confessed that his behaviour makes her feel uncomfortable, but she does not want to risk jeopardising the employee's future, especially since he has only just joined the company. Another female staff member claims that the next time he does it, she will 'give him a smack'. What do you do?

1. Take the new employee to one side and tell him that his behaviour needs to change.

Efficient | Fairly Efficient | Inefficient | Counterproductive

2. Go to your manager and explain the situation.

Efficient | Fairly Efficient | Inefficient | Counterproductive

3. Encourage your female colleagues to speak to your manager.

Efficient | Fairly Efficient | Inefficient | Counterproductive

4. Ignore the behaviour. He's only joking.

Efficient | Fairly Efficient | Inefficient | Counterproductive

Q4.

> You have been working in a hugely successful company for the past 10 years. Recently, however, profits are at an all-time low, employees seem to be drastically underperforming and your sales manager refuses to accept any of the blame. He claims that the bad results are out of his control, and that the products being produced are simply of poor quality. During a recent team meeting, one of your colleagues tried to raise her concerns. Your sales manager lambasted her, branding her weak and naïve. Your colleague was extremely upset by this behaviour, and is considering making a complaint of sexism to the chairman of the company. Although in your opinion there is no evidence to suggest this, she has asked you to act as a witness to her statement. What do you do?

1. Agree to act as a witness, but tell the chairman that there is no evidence to suggest sexism.

Efficient | Fairly Efficient | Inefficient | Counterproductive

2. Tell the chairman that you believe your sales manager was acting in a sexist manner.

Efficient | Fairly Efficient | Inefficient | Counterproductive

3. Agree to act a witness. Suggest to the chairman that the department needs some extra help.

Efficient | Fairly Efficient | Inefficient | Counterproductive

4. Encourage your colleague to sue the company. Sexism is unacceptable.

Efficient | Fairly Efficient | Inefficient | Counterproductive

Q5.

> You are working for a train company as a platform assistant. Part of your job is to assist disabled passengers on and off the train. It is the middle of a weekday, and therefore there are very few customers to deal with. On the other side of the platform, you notice a well-known celebrity. One of your colleagues has noticed this too, and suggests that you both go over to the other side to get her autograph. What do you do?

1. Agree to cross over and get an autograph. This could be your only chance to meet such a prestigious person.

Efficient | Fairly Efficient | Inefficient | Counterproductive

2. Tell your colleague that you won't be going anywhere. What they do is up to them.

Efficient | Fairly Efficient | Inefficient | Counterproductive

3. Refuse to go, and encourage your colleague to do the same. This would be unprofessional.

Efficient | Fairly Efficient | Inefficient | Counterproductive

4. Take photos of the celebrity from afar, but don't approach them.

Efficient | Fairly Efficient | Inefficient | Counterproductive

Q6.

> You are the customer service assistant in a shopping centre. Two men approach you, arguing furiously. One of the men is claiming that the other man took his bag. The other man says that the bag was his all along, and that the first man is lying. He states 'finder's keepers'. You ask the man to hand over the bag to you, so that the CCTV footage of the centre can be reviewed. This leaves the first man irate. As you turn around to deal with him, the second man runs off with the bag, jumps into a taxi, and is gone. What do you do?

1. Offer to take the man's contact details, so that he can be reimbursed for the price of some of his shopping.

Efficient | Fairly Efficient | Inefficient | Counterproductive

2. Tell the man there is nothing that can be done. You snooze, you lose.

Efficient | Fairly Efficient | Inefficient | Counterproductive

3. Report the incident to senior management. Tell the man that your company will be in touch.

Efficient | Fairly Efficient | Inefficient | Counterproductive

4. Take the man into a private room where you can write up a report of the incident, which will then be passed on to the police.

Efficient | Fairly Efficient | Inefficient | Counterproductive

Q7.

> You are working as a barista in a coffee shop. Every Tuesday, a man comes in your shop at 10am. You have noticed that he wears a wedding ring. He sits at the same table, in the same seat, every time. The man often brings female companions with him, and appears very affectionate to all of them. In the past 2 months, you have seen the man kiss at least 5 different women. You suspect him of cheating. What do you do?

1. Ignore the situation. It's none of your business.

   Efficient | Fairly Efficient | Inefficient | Counterproductive

2. Confront the man on the spot. Cheating is immoral.

   Efficient | Fairly Efficient | Inefficient | Counterproductive

3. Take the man to one side and quietly ask him to explain his behaviour.

   Efficient | Fairly Efficient | Inefficient | Counterproductive

4. Talk to your colleague about your concern, this is a good outlet.

   Efficient | Fairly Efficient | Inefficient | Counterproductive

Q8.

You are the centre manager for a well-known writing retreat in the English countryside. Part of your role is ensuring that the centre is well staffed, food goes out on time and that the centre is kept clean and tidy. You have recently taken on a new staff member, who is struggling with his position. Today you have discovered that the new staff member has forgotten to pre-order food supplies, meaning that there is no way to cook dinner for the course attendees that evening. The staff member is fairly upset at his mistake. What do you say to him?

1. 'Pack your bags. You're sacked.'

Efficient | Fairly Efficient | Inefficient | Counterproductive

2. 'Mistakes happen. Let's pull the team together and brainstorm some ideas as to how we can fix this.'

Efficient | Fairly Efficient | Inefficient | Counterproductive

3. 'Maybe you should consider whether this is the right position for you.'

Efficient | Fairly Efficient | Inefficient | Counterproductive

4. 'Okay, obviously this isn't ideal, but let's think of some solutions. We'll have a serious chat about this at the end of the day though.'

Efficient | Fairly Efficient | Inefficient | Counterproductive

Q9.

You are the manager of a major sporting retail store. The previous day, one of your staff members was using a ladder to retrieve an item for a customer. Due to incorrect safety precautions, the ladder fell, injuring the staff member. She has broken her ankle, and therefore won't be in work for a significant period of time. It is your job to call her the next day. What do you say to her?

1. 'Hi. I'm really sorry about the incident that occurred yesterday. We hope to see you back at work soon.'

Efficient │ Fairly Efficient │ Inefficient │ Counterproductive

2. 'Hi. Unfortunately, since you are part time, and can no longer work, we are going to have to terminate your contract.'

Efficient │ Fairly Efficient │ Inefficient │ Counterproductive

3. 'Hi. Do you think you could come in and work on crutches?'

Efficient │ Fairly Efficient │ Inefficient │ Counterproductive

4. 'Hi. I'm really sorry about the incident that took place at work yesterday. I'd like to assure you that we will conduct a full investigation of the incident, to ensure it doesn't happen again.'

Efficient │ Fairly Efficient │ Inefficient │ Counterproductive

Q10.

You are a staff member at a care home. You recently took a week off for a relative's funeral. Upon your return to the care home, you hear that your manager has been gossiping about you behind your back, with the other staff at the care home. According to your source, your manager questioned the necessity of taking 5 days off for a funeral, and called you lazy. You are upset by these claims. What do you do?

1. Spread bad rumours about your manager. Two can play that game.

Efficient | Fairly Efficient | Inefficient | Counterproductive

2. Take your manager to one side and question her on whether the claims are true. Explain why you needed the time off.

Efficient | Fairly Efficient | Inefficient | Counterproductive

3. Arrange a team meeting to try and get to the bottom of this.

Efficient | Fairly Efficient | Inefficient | Counterproductive

4. Ring your manager in your own time to try and discuss the situation further.

Efficient | Fairly Efficient | Inefficient | Counterproductive

Answers

Q1.

1. Say no. You are already settled in at your desk and to move would cause unnecessary upheaval.

Answer: Counterproductive

Explanation: This is counterproductive. The lady is disabled and by not agreeing to her request you are failing to help improve her working environment. By choosing this option you will also serve to deteriorate your working relationship with both her and the rest of your team.

2. Say yes. This is not a problem for you and you can see why moving desks would help her out and improve her working day.

Answer: Efficient

Explanation: This is efficient. Not only does it improve her working environment, it also serves to improve/enhance relations within the office environment.

3. Tell her to speak to your boss first, to see if he is in agreement with her request. If he doesn't have a problem with it, neither do you.

Answer: Fairly Efficient

Explanation: This is fairly efficient, simply because you are informing your boss of what the proposed plan is regarding swapping desks.

4. Tell her you would be willing to swap desks providing she is prepared to move all of your belongings to the new desk.

Answer: Inefficient

Explanation: This is inefficient. Although you have agreed to the desk swap, the lady is in a wheelchair and may not be capable of moving all of your office belongings.

Q2.

1. Consult with the other people in the carriage as to what to do.

Answer: Inefficient

Explanation: This is unprofessional. It's nothing to do with the other people in the carriage, and they shouldn't have to tell you how to do your job.

2. Allow him to pay the full ticket fare to his intended stop.

Answer: Fairly Efficient

Explanation: This is fairly efficient, in the sense that you are showing compassion and common sense. However, technically the man is breaking the law by travelling without buying a ticket first. It could be argued that you should fine him. If everyone made this excuse and bought their tickets on the train instead, train operating companies could lose hundreds of thousands of pounds. There is also no way to ascertain whether he is lying about what stop he boarded at.

3. Perform a citizen's arrest. This man is a criminal.

Answer: Counterproductive

Explanation: This is counterproductive. The man has done nothing to warrant a citizen's arrest, and certainly does not appear to be dangerous or in need of restraint.

4. Issue the man with a standard penalty fare.

Answer: Efficient

Explanation: Regardless of his personal circumstances, the man has broken the rules, and therefore you need to issue him with a penalty fare.

Q3.

1. Take the new employee to one side and tell him that his behaviour needs to change.

Answer: Fairly Efficient

Explanation: This is a fairly efficient response. You are taking steps to try and amend the situation, without going to management straight away. By discussing it with the new employee to one side, you are not humiliating him in front of your other colleagues.

2. Go to your manager and explain the situation.

Answer: Inefficient

Explanation: This is an inefficient response, as the woman has already said that she does not want to jeopardise the employee's position at the company. Therefore it is not up to you to go to management.

3. Encourage your female colleagues to speak to your manager.

Answer: Efficient

Explanation: This is efficient, as it is the right thing to do. Although you should of course take some responsibility for helping your colleagues, ultimately it is their issue to take to the manager.

4. Ignore the behaviour. He's only joking.

Answer: Counterproductive

Explanation: This is counterproductive. Sexual harassment/ inappropriateness is a serious issue.

Q4.

1. Agree to act as a witness, but tell the chairman that there is no evidence to suggest sexism.

Answer: Efficient

Explanation: This is efficient, as it is an honest response. If you have not seen any evidence of sexism, then you cannot support these claims. All you need to do is tell the chairman what you saw.

2. Tell the chairman that you believe your sales manager was acting in a sexist manner.

Answer: Inefficient

Explanation: This is inefficient. As the passage states, you have seen no evidence of sexism.

3. Agree to act a witness. Suggest to the chairman that the department needs some extra help.

Answer: Fairly Efficient

Explanation: This is a fairly efficient response, as you are agreeing to act as a witness, and offering some advice on how to fix other difficult issues. That being said, you haven't been brought into the meeting to discuss the latter.

4. Encourage your colleague to sue the company. Sexism is unacceptable.

Answer: Counterproductive

Explanation: This is counterproductive. Not only have you seen no evidence of sexism, but suing the company would be a fairly extreme course of action.

Q5.

1. Agree to cross over and get an autograph. This could be your only chance to meet such a prestigious author.

Answer: Counterproductive

Explanation: This is counterproductive. It would be extremely unprofessional to abandon your post just to go and get an autograph. Furthermore, the celebrity might not want to be harassed.

2. Tell your colleague that you won't be going anywhere. What they do is up to them.

Answer: Fairly Efficient

Explanation: This demonstrates that you are following the rules and standards expected of you. You are not the keeper of your other colleague, so you cannot force them to stay.

3. Refuse to go, and encourage your colleague to do the same. This would be unprofessional.

Answer: Efficient

Explanation: This is efficient. It would be extremely unprofessional to abandon your post just to go and get an autograph. Furthermore, the person might not want to be harassed. The fact that you have encouraged your colleague to do the same shows that you are thinking in the best interests of the company.

4. Take photos of the celebrity from afar, but don't approach them.

Answer: Inefficient

Explanation: This is an inefficient response. Although you aren't leaving your post, you are acting unprofessionally.

Q6.

1. Offer to take the man's contact details, so that he can be reimbursed for the price of some of his shopping.

Answer: Inefficient

Explanation: This is inefficient. The man does not need to be reimbursed for his shopping, he just wants his bag back.

2. Tell the man there is nothing that can be done. You snooze, you lose.

Answer: Counterproductive

Explanation: This is counterproductive. You are being extremely unsympathetic and unprofessional, along with refusing to take any responsibility.

3. Report the incident to senior management. Tell the man that your company will be in touch.

Answer: Fairly Efficient

Explanation: This is fairly efficient, as it demonstrates that you are taking reasonable action in order to resolve the issue. Whilst you have been quite vague in terms of getting in contact with him, it still shows that you are acting upon it by going to management.

4. Take the man into a private room where you can write up a report of the incident, which will then be passed on to the police.

Answer: Efficient

Explanation: This is efficient, as it means that you have taken initiative, acted in a responsible manner and then passed the matter over to the organisation best equipped to deal with it. Along with this, you have made the man feel reassured that the case is in good hands.

Q7.

1. Ignore the situation. It's none of your business.

Answer: Efficient

Explanation: This is an efficient response. Customer personal matters are nothing to do with staff, provided they aren't breaking laws or rules.

2. Confront the man on the spot. Cheating is immoral.

Answer: Counterproductive

Explanation: This is a counterproductive response. Regardless of how you feel about the man's behaviour, it's none of your business.

3. Take the man to one side and quietly ask him to explain his behaviour.

Answer: Inefficient

Explanation: This is an inefficient response. Once again, it is none of your business, and you would be acting unprofessionally.

4. Talk to your colleague about your concern, this is a good outlet.

Answer: Fairly Efficient

Explanation: This is a fairly efficient response, as it allows you to discuss the issue without it having an impact on the business.

Q8.

1. 'Pack your bags. You're sacked.'

Answer: Counterproductive

Explanation: Sacking the employee on the spot won't solve anything, and would be unprofessional.

2. 'Mistakes happen. Let's pull the team together and brainstorm some ideas as to how we can fix this.'

Answer: Efficient

Explanation: This is efficient as it allows you to try and reach a positive solution to the situation, whilst gaining suggestions from a wide variety of people.

3. 'Maybe you should consider whether this is the right position for you.'

Answer: Inefficient

Explanation: This is an inefficient response. There will be time to discuss this after the incident has been resolved. All this will do is damage the employee's confidence, making him less likely to successfully complete future tasks.

4. 'Okay, obviously this isn't ideal, but let's think of some solutions. We'll have a serious chat about this at the end of the day though.'

Answer: Fairly Efficient

Explanation: This is a fairly efficient response. You are treating the issue in a constructive manner, but still ensuring that the employee knows that it's a serious mistake.

Q9.

1. 'Hi. I'm really sorry about the incident that occurred yesterday. We hope to see you back at work soon.'

Answer: Fairly Efficient

Explanation: This is fairly efficient, because it shows a willingness to take responsibility for the incident and a level of care for the employee. However, you have failed to make reassurances that the incident is being looked into.

2. 'Hi. Unfortunately, since you are part time, and can no longer work, we are going to have to terminate your contract.'

Answer: Counterproductive

Explanation: This is counterproductive. It shows a lack of care and professionalism, and is completely unfair on the employee, particularly since it was the company's fault to begin with.

3. 'Hi. Do you think you could come in and work on crutches?'

Answer: Inefficient

Explanation: This is inefficient. The employee is obviously unable to continue working on crutches and therefore this would not benefit them or the company.

4. 'Hi. I'm really sorry about the incident that took place at work yesterday. I'd like to assure you that we will conduct a full investigation of the incident, to ensure it doesn't happen again.'

Answer: Efficient

Explanation: This is an efficient response to the situation. You are making clear reassurances that the problem will be looked into, and apologising to the employee.

Q10.

1. Spread bad rumours about your manager. Two can play that game.

Answer: Counterproductive

Explanation: This is counterproductive. It is extremely unprofessional, and could only lead to more trouble. You should be the better person.

2. Take your manager to one side and question her on whether the claims are true. Explain why you needed the time off.

Answer: Efficient

Explanation: This is efficient, as it constitutes the most reasonable response. It shows both professionalism and integrity.

3. Arrange a team meeting to try and to get to the bottom of this.

Answer: Inefficient

Explanation: This is an inefficient response, as you are involving your colleagues in a situation between you and your manager. You should be aiming to stop them gossiping or getting involved, therefore conducting a meeting will only make the situation worse.

4. Ring your manager in your own time to try and discuss the situation further.

Answer: Fairly Efficient

Explanation: This is a fairly efficient response, as it shows that you are looking to try and resolve the situation in a positive manner.

Mechanical Aptitude

Mechanical comprehension or aptitude tests have been in use for many years. They are used to assess a candidate's potential to perform a specific job. Many mechanical comprehension tests require you to concentrate on 'principles' rather than on making calculations, and as such will include diagrams and pictures as part of the question.

For example, you may be shown a diagram of a series of cogs. You will be asked to work out which way a specific cog is turning, if another one rotates either clockwise or anti-clockwise. Understanding these two very simple terms is crucial to answering mechanical comprehension test questions accurately. For those people who are unsure, here's an explanation:

CLOCKWISE AND ANTI-CLOCKWISE

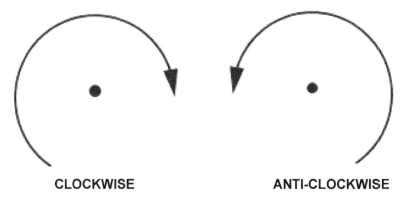

CLOCKWISE   ANTI-CLOCKWISE

The easiest way to remember the above is to think of the way that the hands on a clock rotate; hence the phrase 'clockwise'.

You may also find that some test questions, which have been created in the USA, refer to anti-clockwise as 'counter-clockwise'.

UNDERSTANDING MECHANICAL ADVANTAGE

Some mechanical comprehension tests ask you to calculate the mechanical advantage of a simple pulley system.

Here's an explanation of how mechanical advantage works when using a simple pulley system.

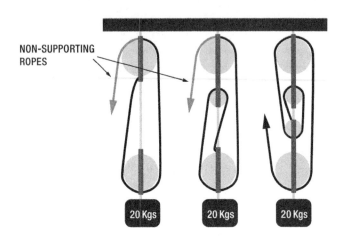

EXAMPLES OF SIMPLE PULLEY SYSTEMS

If you study the three pulley systems above, you will note that each system has both supporting ropes and non-supporting ropes. Supporting ropes are ones which, as the name suggests, support the load. Only the first two pulley systems have non-supporting ropes which we have indicated.

The non-supporting ropes in the first two pulley systems above simply change the direction of the force.

To calculate the mechanical advantage in a moveable pulley system, we simply have to count the number of supporting ropes. Counting the supporting ropes in the pulley systems above, the mechanical advantage of each of system is, from left to right 2, 3, and 5.

Now have a go at some sample questions!

Question 1

In the following cog and belt system, which cog will rotate the most number of times in an hour?

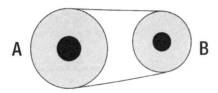

A	B	C
Cog A	Cog B	All the same

Question 2

In the following cog and belt system, which cog will rotate the least number of times in thirty minutes?

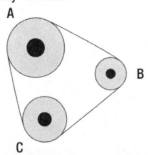

A	B	C
Cog A	Cog B	Cog C

Question 3

Which rope would require the most effort to pull the mast over?

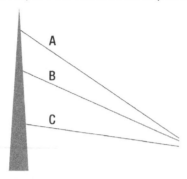

A	B	C
Rope A	Rope B	Rope C

Question 4

If cog A turns anti-clockwise, which way will cog C turn?

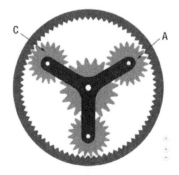

A	B	C
Clockwise	Anti-clockwise	Backwards and forwards

Question 5

What will happen to the air resistance on a car as the car picks up speed?

A	B	C
The air resistance will increase	The air resistance will decrease	The air resistance will stay the same

Question 6

If wheel B moves clockwise at a speed of 20 rpm, how will wheel D move and at what speed?

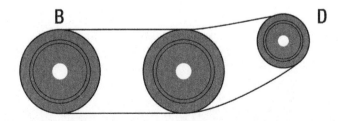

A	B	C	D
Clockwise, more rpm	Clockwise, less rpm	Anti-clockwise, more rpm	Anti-clockwise, less rpm

Question 7

Which is the best tool to use for breaking up concrete?

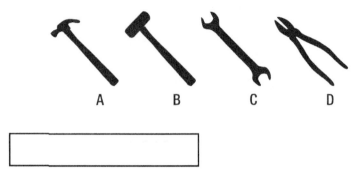

A   B   C   D

Question 8

In the following circuit, if switch A closes and switch B remains open, what will happen?

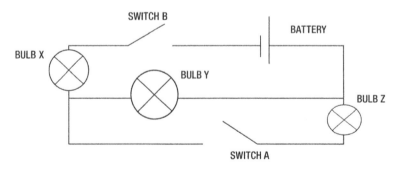

A. Bulbs X, Y and Z will illuminate.

B. Bulb X will illuminate.

C. Bulbs Y and Z will illuminate.

D. No bulbs will illuminate.

Question 9

In the following circuit, if switch A closes, what will happen?

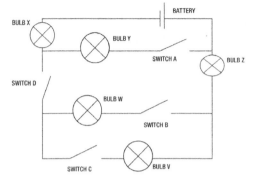

A. Bulbs V, W, X, Y and Z will illuminate.

B. Bulbs X and Y will illuminate.

C. Bulbs X, Y and Z will illuminate.

D. No bulbs will illuminate.

Question 10

Which of the following equations would you use to work out the voltage?

A. Voltage = current ÷ resistance

B. Voltage = resistance ÷ current

C. Voltage = current × resistance

D. Voltage = power × resistance

Answers

Q1. B

Cog B is smaller and therefore will rotate more times in the given timeframe.

Q2. A

Because cog A is the largest of the three cogs it will rotate fewer times for any given timeframe.

Q3. C

The higher up the mast the rope is secured, the easier it will be to pull it over. This is because there is more leverage than a rope secured towards the bottom of the mast. Therefore, rope C will require the most effort.

Q4. B

Cog C will rotate anti-clockwise.

Q5. A

As the car picks up speed, the air resistance will increase.

Q6. A

Wheel D will rotate clockwise, but because it is smaller in size it will rotate more rpm than B.

Q7. B

Both A and B are suitable for breaking up concrete, however, B (sledge hammer) is designed specifically for this purpose.

Q8. D

Because the second switch is still open, the circuit will remain broken and therefore no bulbs will illuminate.

Q9. B

Only bulbs X and Y can illuminate in this circuit because the remaining switches remain open.

Q10. C

In order to work out the voltage, you must multiply the current of the circuit by the resistance.

Fault Finding

When working on an offshore rig, a large part of your role will be in fault finding and error checking. Regular maintenance on your equipment, and on the offshore systems, is integral. With this in mind, we have devised a short test to replicate this. The questions are based on switches. Your task is to identify which of the switches is not working. The box on the left side contains four circles, each labelled A, B, C and D.

A key to the switches and the function that they perform is detailed below.

Which switch in the sequence is not working?

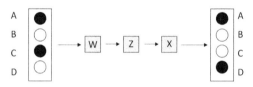

SWITCH   FUNCTION OF THE SWITCH

W   Turns A and C on/off
           i.e. Black to white and vice versa

X   Turns B and D on/off
           i.e. Black to white and vice versa

Y   Turns C and D on/off
           i.e. Black to white and vice versa

Z   Turns A and D on/off
           i.e. Black to white and vice versa

You will notice that the box on the left side contains black circles A and C, and white circled B and D at the start of the sequence. The first switch to operate is 'W', which has the effect of turning circles A and C from black to white, and vice versa. Once switch 'W' operates, the lights on the left will all be white.

The next switch to operate is switch Z, which has the effect of turning circles A and D from black to white and vice versa. Because the circles contained within the box on the left side are all white after the operation of switch W, this now means that circles A and D are black, and circles B and C are white.

You will notice that the box with the four circles located on the right side is now identical to this, which means that the next switch, switch X must be inoperative. If it was working correctly, then the box of circles on the right side would look different. Therefore, the correct answer to the question is Switch X.

Question 1

Which switch in the sequence is not working?

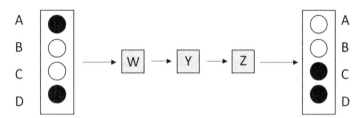

SWITCH   FUNCTION OF THE SWITCH

W   Turns A and C on/off
Y   Turns C and D on/off
Z   Turns A and D on/off

Answer

Question 2

Which switch in the sequence is not working?

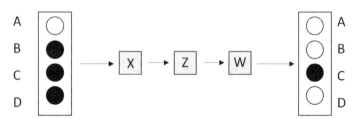

SWITCH   FUNCTION OF THE SWITCH

W   Turns A and C on/off
X   Turns B and D on/off
Z   Turns A and D on/off

Answer

Question 3

Which switch in the sequence is not working?

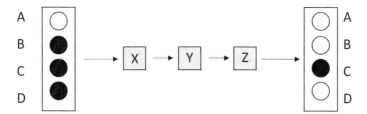

SWITCH   FUNCTION OF THE SWITCH

X   Turns B and D on/off
Y   Turns C and D on/off
Z   Turns A and D on/off

Answer

Question 4

Which switch in the sequence is not working?

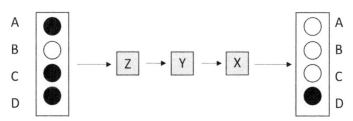

SWITCH   FUNCTION OF THE SWITCH

X   Turns B and D on/off
Y   Turns C and D on/off
Z   Turns A and D on/off

Answer

Question 5

Which switch in the sequence is not working?

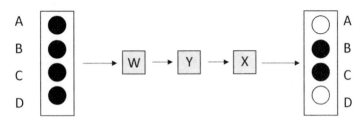

SWITCH   FUNCTION OF THE SWITCH

W   Turns A and C on/off
X   Turns B and D on/off
Y   Turns C and D on/off

Answer

Question 6

Which switch in the sequence is not working?

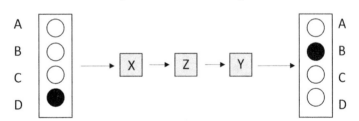

SWITCH   FUNCTION OF THE SWITCH

X   Turns B and D on/off
Y   Turns C and D on/off
Z   Turns A and D on/off

Answer

Question 7

Which switch in the sequence is not working?

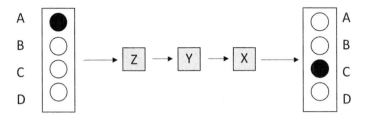

SWITCH   FUNCTION OF THE SWITCH

X   Turns B and D on/off
Y   Turns C and D on/off
Z   Turns A and D on/off

Answer

Question 8

Which switch in the sequence is not working?

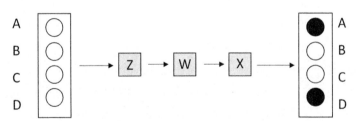

SWITCH   FUNCTION OF THE SWITCH

W   Turns A and C on/off
X   Turns B and D on/off
Z   Turns A and D on/off

Answer

Question 9

Which switch in the sequence is not working?

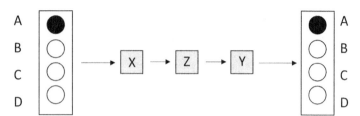

SWITCH   FUNCTION OF THE SWITCH

X   Turns B and D on/off
Y   Turns C and D on/off
Z   Turns A and D on/off

Answer

Question 10

Which switch in the sequence is not working?

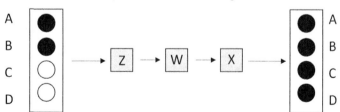

SWITCH   FUNCTION OF THE SWITCH

W   Turns A and C on/off
X   Turns B and D on/off
Z   Turns A and D on/off

Answer

Answers

Q1. Switch Y

EXPLANATION = the first switch to operate is 'W', which has the effect of turning circles A and C from black to white, and vice versa. Once switch 'W' operates, circles C and D will be black. You will notice that the box on the right side is now identical to this, which means the next switch, switch Y, must be inoperative.

Q2. Switch Z

EXPLANATION = the first switch to operate is 'X', which has the effect of turning circles B and D from black to white, and vice versa. Once switch 'X' operates, circle B changes from black to white, and circle D changes from black to white. (This gives you the image on the right). You will notice that the box on the right side is now identical to this, which means the next switch, switch Z, must be inoperative.

Q3. Switch Y

EXPLANATION = the first switch to operate is 'X', which has the effect of turning circles B and D from black to white, and vice versa. Once switch 'X' operates, circle C is the only circle that is black. You will notice that the box on the right side is now identical to this, which means the next switch, switch Y, must be inoperative.

Q4. Switch X

EXPLANATION = the first switch to operate is 'Z', which has the effect of turning circles A and D from black to white, and vice versa. Once switch 'Z' operates, only circle C will be black. The next switch to operate is switch Y, which has the effect of turning circles C and D from black to white and vice versa. Once switch Y operates, only circle D will be black. You will notice that the box on the right side is now identical to this, which means the next switch, switch X, must be inoperative.

Q5. Switch X

EXPLANATION = the first switch to operate is 'W', which has the effect of turning circles A and C from black to white, and vice versa. Once switch 'W' operates, only circles B and D will be black. The next switch to operate is switch Y, which has the effect of turning circles C and D from black to white, and vice versa. Once switch Y operates, only circles B and C will be black. You will notice that the box on the right side is now identical to this, which means the next switch, switch X, must be inoperative.

Q6. Switch Z

EXPLANATION = the first switch to operate is 'X', which has the effect of turning circles B and D from black to white, and vice versa. Once switch 'X' operates, only circle B will be black. You will notice that the box on the right side is now identical to this, which means the next switch, switch Z, must be inoperative.

Q7. Switch X

EXPLANATION = the first switch to operate is 'Z', which has the effect of turning circles A and D from black to white, and vice versa. Once switch 'Z' operates, only circle D will be black. The next switch to operate is switch 'Y', which has the effect of turning circles C and D from black to white, and vice versa. Once switch 'Y' operates, only circle C will be black. You will notice that the box on the right side is now identical to this, which means the next switch, switch X, must be inoperative.

Q8. Switch W

EXPLANATION = the first switch to operate is 'Z', which has the effect of turning circles A and D from black to white, and vice versa. Once switch 'Z' operates, only circles A and D will be black. You will notice that the box on the right side is now identical to this, which means the next switch, switch W, must be inoperative.

Q9. Switch X

EXPLANATION = the first switch to operate is 'X', which has the effect of turning circles B and D from black to white, and vice versa. You will notice that the start of the sequence has only circle A that is black; and this is identical to the end of the sequence, whereby only circle A is black. This means that the first switch in the sequence, switch X, must be inoperative.

Q10. Switch X

EXPLANATION = the first switch to operate is 'Z', which has the effect of turning circles A and D from black to white, and vice versa. Once switch 'Z' operates, only circles B and D will be black. The next switch to operate is 'W', which has the effect of turning circles A and C from black to white, and vice versa. Once switch 'W' operates, all of the circles will be black. You will notice that the box on the right side is now identical to this, which means the next switch, switch X, must be inoperative.

Verbal Reasoning

Verbal Reasoning or Verbal Ability tests are specifically designed to assess a candidate's ability to reason with words, language or comprehension, and demonstrate a solid understanding of written information within the English language.

The ability to spell words correctly, use correct grammar and punctuation, understand word meanings, and interpret written information, is an imperative skill that is required in a range of situations and job roles. Thus, it is important that you are able to demonstrate these skills to a high standard and perform to the best of your ability.

Most employers who use psychometric tests in job selection processes will include a Verbal Reasoning or Verbal Ability test of some form. This is because there are very few graduate careers which don't require the ability to understand, analyse and interpret written information, often of a complex or specialised nature. Therefore, it is important that recruiters hire a candidate who shows strong levels of verbal and literary ability.

Verbal Ability tests have become increasingly popular for a whole range of career selection processes. Doctors, dentists, police officers, and even pupils who wish to undertake the 11+ test, are all required to sit a Verbal test.

Verbal Reasoning tests come in different formats. Be sure to find out what type of test it is you are going to be sitting. This will help you to practice the questions to the best of your ability. Even if you are required to sit a particular test, i.e a Verbal Comprehension test, it is best to practice a range of Verbal tests to ensure that you are ready for anything that might be used in your actual assessment.

Typical formats of the Verbal test include:

- Verbal Logical Reasoning;
- Verbal Reasoning;
- Verbal Comprehension;
- Vocabulary test;
- Spelling and Grammar test;
- Word Meanings test;
- Word Relations test.

In order for you to gain the best knowledge and practice, the following testing sections will include a variety of question types to ensure you are fully prepared for any Verbal Ability test that you may be required to sit.

Question 1

Which word does not have a similar meaning to – imaginary?

A	B	C	D
Apocryphal	Fictional	Illusory	Inconsistent

Question 2

Which word does not have a similar meaning to – important?

A	B	C	D
Miniature	Significant	Imperative	Of substance

Question 3

Which word does not have a similar meaning to – belittle?

A	B	C	D
Trivialise	Denigrate	Overrate	Malign

Question 4

Which word does not have a similar meaning to – conclusion?

A	B	C	D
Outcome	Upshot	Denouement	Cause

Question 5

Which word is the odd one out?

A	B	C	D	E
Beef	Mutton	Cow	Pork	Ham

Question 6

Which word is the odd one out?

A	B	C	D	E
London	Paris	Lisbon	Prague	Nuremberg

Question 7

Which word is the odd one out?

A	B	C	D	E
Rose	Lily	Daisy	Petal	Sunflower

Question 8

Which word is the odd one out?

A	B	C	D	E
Hungry	Ravenous	Famished	Esurient	Stuffed

Question 9

Which word is the odd one out?

A	B	C	D	E
Ostrich	Parrots	Penguins	Dodo	Owls

Question 10

Find two words, one from each group, that are the closest in meaning.

Group A	Group B
Abysmal, placid, exhausted	Energetic, docile, wonderful

A	B	C	D
Exhausted and docile	Placid and docile	Abysmal and docile	Placid and wonderful

Question 11

Find two words, one from each group, that are the closest in meaning.

Group A	Group B
Confused, enraged, terrified	Calm, trance, incensed

A	B	C	D
Enraged and incensed	Confused and calm	Confused and trance	Terrified and trance

Question 12

Find two words, one from each group, that are the closest in meaning.

Group A	Group B
Determined, frightened, informal	Normal, resolute, unravelling

A	B	C	D
Determined and resolute	Determined and unravelling	Frightened and unravelling	Informal and normal

Question 13

Find two words, one from each group, that are the closest in meaning.

Group A	Group B
Gratitude, shy, courageous	Bold, audacious, friendly

A	B	C	D
Shy and friendly	Gratitude and friendly	Courageous and audacious	Gratitude and bold

Question 14

Which 3 of the 8 three-letter 'bits' can be combined to create a word meaning "having been deserted or left"?

aba, del, tru, ndo, mne, ned, fli, ing

Answer

Question 15

Which 3 of the 8 three-letter 'bits' can be combined to create a word meaning "the use of icons to represent something", or "something can be referred to in linguistic terms"?

bet, bol, bal, ism, pre, ing, sym, rai

Answer

Question 16

Which 3 of the 8 three-letter 'bits' can be combined to create a word meaning "incorrectly positioned or temporarily lost?"

ten, pla, tra, mis, als, ing, ced, den

Answer

Question 17

Which 3 of the 8 three-letter 'bits' can be combined to create a word meaning "the muscle associated with the abdomen"?

tre, ple, omi, art, abd, wre, ing, nal

Answer

Question 18

In the line below, the word outside of the brackets will only go with three of the words inside the brackets to make longer words. Which one word will it not go with?

	A	B	C	D
Un	(alike)	(adjusted)	(capable)	(affected)

Question 19

In the line below, the word outside of the brackets will only go with three of the words inside the brackets to make longer words. Which one word will it not go with?

	A	B	C	D
In	(appropriate)	(justice)	(ethical)	(animate)

Question 20

In the line below, the word outside of the brackets will only go with three of the words inside the brackets to make longer words. Which one word will it not go with?

	A	B	C	D
Down	(out)	(size)	(ward)	(load)

Question 21

In the line below, the word outside of the brackets will only go with three of the words inside the brackets to make longer words. Which one word will it not go with?

	A	B	C	D
In	(decisive)	(reference)	(destructible)	(convenience)

Question 22

Rubbish is to bin as bread is to...?

A	B	C	D
Breadbin	Knife	Buy	Wheat

Question 23

In each question, there are two pairs of words. Only one of the answers will go equally well with both these pairs.

(Tree   Stem)   (Growl   Woof)

A	B	C	D
Cover	Branch	Bark	Dog

Question 24

Peter won an award for outstanding achievement. He _____ the award _____ .

A	B	C	D
excepted / grascious	accepted / graciously	expected / gracily	eccepted / graciously

Question 25

The evidence _____ the jury to reach a unanimous _____ .

A	B	C	D
led / decisive	lead / decision	led / decision	leed / decishion

Question 26

The _____ of the school enforced many _____ to ensure an effective code of conduct.

A	B	C	D
principal / principles	principles / principal	princepal / principals	principle / principles

Question 27

She _____ the piano every day. _____ makes perfect.

A	B	C	D
practices / practices	practices / practices	practises / practice	practises/ practisce

Question 28

Which sentence is written correctly?

A – We will be in contact with you shortly.

B – We will be in contact with you shortley.

C – We will in contact be with you shortly.

D – Shortly will we be in contact with you.

Answer [   ]

Question 29

Which phrase is written correctly?

A – Yours sincerity

B – Your's sincerely

C – Yours sincerely

D – You're sincerely

Answer

Question 30

Which sentence is written correctly?

A – I regret to inform you that you did not get chosen for the internship.

B – I inform to regret you that you did not get chosen for the internship.

C – I regret to inform you, that, you did not get chose for the internship.

D – I regret to inform your that you did not get chosen for the internship.

Answer

Answers

Q1. D = inconsistent

EXPLANATION = the term 'imaginary' can be defined as "existing only in the imagination". The words apocryphal, fictional and illusory, all carry the same connotations as 'imaginary'. Inconsistent is a term used to describe something that "does not stay the same throughout".

Q2. A = miniature

EXPLANATION = the term 'important' can be defined as "being of great significance". The words significant, imperative and crucial, all carry the same connotations as 'significant'. Miniature is a term used to describe something "on a smaller scale".

Q3. C = overrate

EXPLANATION = the term 'belittle' can be defined as "dismissing someone or something as unimportant". The words trivialise, denigrate, and malign, all carry the same connotations as 'belittle'. Overrate is a term used to describe "a higher opinion of something or someone than is deserved".

Q4. D = cause

EXPLANATION = the other three terms are consequences of a cause, whilst 'cause' is a preceding event.

Q5. C = cow

EXPLANATION = 'cow' is the odd one out because all of the other words refer to a type of meat.

Q6. E = Nuremberg

EXPLANATION = 'Nuremberg' is the odd one out because all of the other words are capital cities, whereas Nuremberg is not a capital city.

Q7. D = petal

EXPLANATION = 'petal' is the odd one out because all of the other words refer to a type of flower, whereas petal is part of a flower.

Q8. E = stuffed

EXPLANATION = 'stuffed' is the odd one out because all of the other words are synonyms for being hungry, whereas stuffed is the opposite of being hungry.

Q9. D = dodo

EXPLANATION = 'dodo' is the odd one out because all of the others are birds that are still alive today. A dodo is extinct.

Q10. B = placid and docile

EXPLANATION = placid and docile are the closest in meaning. Both these words refer to calm, peace and submissiveness, with little movement or activity.

Q11. A = enraged and incensed

EXPLANATION = enraged and incensed are the closest in meaning. Both words refer to being very angry and furious.

Q12. A = determined and resolute

EXPLANATION = determined and resolute are the closest in meaning. Both words refer to being determined and unwavering.

Q13. C = courageous and audacious

EXPLANATION = courageous and audacious are the closest in meaning. Both words refer to willingness to take bold risks; they carry connotations of being bold and daring.

Q14. Abandoned

EXPLANATION = the word that can be created in order to demonstrate something being deserted or left, is abandoned.

Q15. Symbolism

EXPLANATION = the word that can be created in order to represent something through icons, and can be referred to in linguistic terms, is symbolism.

Q16. Misplaced

EXPLANATION = the word that can be created in order to demonstrate something being placed in the incorrect position, or temporarily lost, is misplaced.

Q17. Abdominal

EXPLANATION = the word that can be created in order to demonstrate the muscle associated with the abdomen.

Q18. C = capable

EXPLANATION = unalike, unadjusted, unaffected. Therefore the word that (un) does not go with is capable. (Instead it would be incapable).

Q19. C = ethical

EXPLANATION = inappropriate, injustice, inanimate. Therefore the word that (in) does not go with is ethical. (Instead it would be unethical).

Q20. A = out

EXPLANATION = downsize, downward, download. Therefore the word that (down) does not go with is out. This does not make a word.

Q21. B = reference

EXPLANATION = indecisive, indestructible, inconvenience. Therefore the word that (in) does not go with is reference. Instead this would need to be two separate words i.e. in reference to...

Q22. A = Breadbin

EXPLANATION = rubbish is stored in the bin as bread is stored in the breadbin

Q23. C = bark

EXPLANATION = bark can mean part of a tree, or the bark (woof) sound of a dog.

Q24. B = accepted / graciously

EXPLANATION = accepted and graciously are the correct words in order to fit in with the sentence structure.

Q25. C = led / decision

EXPLANATION = led and decision are the correct words in order to fit in with the sentence structure.

Q26. A = principal / principles

EXPLANATION = principal and principles are the correct words in order to fit in with the sentence structure.

Q27. C = practises / practice

EXPLANATION = practises and practice are the correct words in order to fit in with the sentence structure.

Q28. A = 'We will be in contact with you shortly'.

EXPLANATION = sentence A is the only sentence that is written correctly.

Q29. C = 'Yours sincerely'

EXPLANATION = C is the only phrase that is written correctly.

Q30. A = 'I regret to inform you that you did not get chosen for the internship'.

EXPLANATION = A is the only sentence that is written correctly.

Numerical Reasoning

A Numerical Reasoning test is designed to assess mathematical knowledge through number-related assessments. These assessments will consist of different difficulty levels, and will all vary depending on who you are sitting the test for. Be sure to find out what type of Numerical Reasoning test you will be sitting, to ensure you make the most out of your preparation time.

Numerical Reasoning is one of the most common forms of psychometric testing. It enables employers to filter out strong candidates from those less desirable. Most recruitment processes now contain a form of psychometric and aptitude testing, so it is important that you are 100% prepared!

The majority of Numerical Reasoning tests are administered to candidates who are applying for managerial, graduate and professional positions – any job that deals with making inferences in relation to statistical, financial or numerical data. However, some employers may use these tests as a way of determining important job-related skills such as time management and problem solving efficiency.

Numerical Reasoning tests can be used to assess the following:

- Basic Mental Arithmetic;
- Critical Reasoning;
- General Intelligence ;
- Estimations;
- Speed and Concentration;
- Financial Reasoning;
- Data Analysis.

Numerical Reasoning tests cover a wide range of mathematical formulae. It is imperative to comprehend the skills and knowledge required to work out the mathematics involved. Most Numerical Reasoning tests contain questions in relation to:

Adding	Subtracting	Dividing	Multiplying
Fractions	Percentages	Decimals	Ratios
Charts and Graphs	Mean, Mode, Median, Range	Areas and Perimeters	Number Sequences
Time	Conversions	Measurements	Money
Proportions	Formulae	Data Interpretation	Quantitative Data

During the Numerical Reasoning test, you will have a specific amount of time to answer each question. It is important that you do not spend too much time on one particular question. Remember, the clock is ticking, so if you are stuck on a question, move on and come back to it at the end if you have time.

Question 1

Calculate 4.99 + 19.09

A	B	C	D	E
24.02	28.04	22.08	24.08	22.04

Question 2

Calculate 6.47 − 3.29

A	B	C	D	E
3.12	3.15	4.14	4.16	3.18

Question 3

Multiply 6 by 7 and then divide by 3.

A	B	C	D	E
14	16	12	8	42

Question 4

Divide 120 by 4 and then multiply it by 5.

A	B	C	D	E
200	150	100	50	65

Question 5

What is $\frac{8}{11}$ of 88?

A	B	C	D	E
64	42	48	72	78

Question 6

Calculate 4.8 × 3.0.

A	B	C	D	E
13.6	13.2	14.4	14.8	15.0

Question 7

Calculate 2.2 × 22.2

A	B	C	D	E
84.84	48.48	88.44	48.84	44.88

Question 8

Convert 0.8 to a fraction. In its simplest form.

A	B	C	D	E
$\frac{8}{10}$	$\frac{1}{2}$	$\frac{3}{4}$	$\frac{4}{5}$	$\frac{5}{8}$

Question 9

What is 0.9 as a percentage?

A	B	C	D	E
0.009%	0.9%	9%	90%	19%

Question 10

Using BIDMAS work out 23.7 − 2.5 × 8.

A	B	C	D	E
37	2.7	169.6	3.7	3.2

Question 11

In the following question, what is the value of x?

$$\frac{3x - 6}{5} = 9$$

A	B	C	D	E
13	16	17	19	21

Question 12

Convert $\frac{7}{10}$ to a decimal.

A	B	C	D	E
0.7	7.0	0.07	0.007	7.7

Question 13

If you count from 1 to 100, how many numbers containing the number '4', will you pass on the way?

A	B	C	D	E
21	20	19	11	10

Question 14

Calculate $144 \div 6$.

A	B	C	D	E
21	20	24	26	30

Question 15

What is 75% of 3,200?

A	B	C	D	E
2,600	3,000	3,250	2,400	2,750

Question 16

What is 48% of 900?

A	B	C	D	E
412	432	462	400	480

Question 17

What is 1,888 ÷ 4?

A	B	C	D	E
514	364	394	457	472

Question 18

What is 8 × 4.9?

A	B	C	D	E
33.2	37.2	39.2	31.2	38.2

Question 19

$41 × 9 = 738 ÷ ?$

A	B	C	D	E
5	4	7	2	3

Question 20

A function is represented by the following machine.

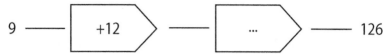

9 is put into the machine. The output of the machine is 126. What is the missing function in the second part of the machine sequence?

A	B	C	D	E
× 12	÷ 12	× 6	÷ 6	− 8

Question 21

Subtract ⅜ of 104 from 5/7 of 98.

A	B	C	D	E
22	28	39	31	37

Question 22

Here is a spinner. Circle the chance of the spinner landing on an odd number.

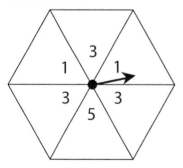

A	B	C	D
6/6 or 1	4/6	1/2	1/3

Question 23

What two numbers come next in the sequence?

2, 4, 8, 16, 32, 64, ...

A	B	C	D
126 and 215	128 and 256	128 and 265	182 and 265

Question 24

Simplify $x + 8x - 3x$.

A	B	C	D
$5x$	$6x$	$7x$	$12x$

Question 25

There are 20 buttons in a bag. 12 are red, 5 are green and the rest are white. A button is chosen at random. Work out the probability that the button will be white.

A	B	C	D
$\frac{3}{20}$	$\frac{1}{5}$	$\frac{3}{10}$	$\frac{9}{20}$

Question 26

On a school trip at least 1 teacher is needed for every 8 students. Work out the minimum number of teachers needed for 138 students.

A	B	C	D
17	14	16	18

Question 27

The sterling to US dollar rate is 1:1.60. How many dollars would you receive if you changed up £450?

A	B	C	D
$490	$720	$780	$650

Question 28

Linda is hiking. Using a compass, she discovers that she is facing west. If she turns 8 right angles clockwise, what way will she be facing?

A	B	C	D
South	North	West	East

Question 29

A family of 4 split the cost of all the household bills equally. The water bill was £80.40, the gas bill was £35.00 and the electric bill was £40.00. The rent for the month was £490. How much does each member of the family put towards covering all the bill costs?

A	B	C	D
£161.25	£191.35	£161.35	£161.50

Question 30

What is 560 ÷ 7?

A	B	C	D
60	90	85	80

Answers

Q1. D = 24.08
EXPLANATION = 4.99 + 19.09 = 24.08

Q2. E = 3.18
EXPLANATION = 6.47 − 3.29 = 3.18

Q3. A = 14
EXPLANATION = 6 × 7 = 42 ÷ 3 = 14

Q4. B = 150
EXPLANATION = 120 ÷ 4 = 30 × 5 = 150

Q5. D = 72
EXPLANATION = 88 ÷ 11 × 9 = 72

Q6. C = 14.4
EXPLANATION = to multiply decimals, it is best to take out the decimal points, do the calculation, and then add them back in after. So, 48 × 3 = 144. Remember, there is one number after the decimal point in the question, so one number needs to be after the decimal point in the answer. So, 144 will become 14.4

Q7. D = 48.84
EXPLANATION = to multiply decimals, it is best to take out the decimal points, do the calculation, and then add them back in after. So, 22 × 222 = 4884. Remember, there are two numbers after the decimal point (one in 2.2 and one in 22.2), so two numbers need to come after the decimal point in the answer. So, 4,884 will become 48.84.

Q8. D = ⅘
EXPLANATION = to convert a decimal into a fraction, it is best to make it a percentage, and then work out the fraction. So, 0.8 ×

100 = 80%. As a decimal 80% is equivalent to $^{80}/_{100}$. This can be simplified to $^4/_5$. Although answer option A is correct, the question specifically asks for the answer in its simplest form, so answer option D would be correct.

Q9. D = 90%
EXPLANATION = 0.9 × 100 = 90%.

Q10. D = 3.7
Following the rule of BIDMAS, you will need to work out the multiplication first. So, 2.5 × 8 = 20.

You can then do the subtraction. So, 23.7 − 20 = 3.7

Q11. C = 17
EXPLANATION = in order to work out the value of x:

9 × 5 = 45 + 6 = 51 ÷ 3 = 17. The important thing to remember is that when you take the number from the top row, you have to do the opposite to what it is saying. so, '−6' becomes '+6'.

Q12. A = 0.7
EXPLANATION = 7 ÷ 10 = 0.7

Q13. C = 19
EXPLANATION = from 1 to 100, you would encounter 19 numbers that contain the number 4.

4, 14, 24, 34, 40, 41, 42, 43, 44, 45, 46, 47, 48, 49, 54, 64, 74, 84, 94.

Q14. C = 24
EXPLANATION = 144 ÷ 6 = 24

Q15. D = 2,400
EXPLANATION = 3,200 ÷ 100 × 75 = 2,400

Q16. B = 432
EXPLANATION = 900 ÷ 100 × 48 = 432

Q17. E = 472
EXPLANATION = 1,888 ÷ 4 = 472

Q18. C = 39.2
EXPLANATION = to multiply decimals, it is best to take out the decimal points, do the calculation, and then add them back in after. So, 8 × 49 = 392. Remember, there is one number after the decimal point in the question, so there needs to be one number after the decimal point in the answer. So, 392 will become 39.2.

Q19. D = 2
EXPLANATION = 41 × 9 = 369 which is the same as 738 ÷ 2 = 369.

Q20. C = × 6
EXPLANATION = 9 + 12 = 21. 126 ÷ 21 = 6. Therefore if you put (×6) into the equation (because you divided 126 by 6, you would put the opposite into the equation). Therefore, 9 + 12 × 6 = 126.

Q21. D = 31
EXPLANATION = 104 ÷ 8 × 3 = 39.　　98 ÷ 7 × 5 = 70.
So, 70 – 39 = 31.

Q22. A = ⁶⁄₆ or 1.
EXPLANATION = the spinner contains only odd numbers. So no matter what number it lands on, you will always spin an odd number.

Q23. B = 128 and 256
EXPLANATION = the sequence follows the pattern of multiplying by 2 each time. So, 64 × 2 = 128 and 128 × 2 = 256.

Q24. B = 6x
EXPLANATION = x + 8x = 9x.　　So, 9x – 3x = 6x.

Q25. A = ³⁄₂₀

EXPLANATION = 20 − 12 − 5 = 3. So your chance of picking a white button is 3 out of a possible 20.

Q26. D = 18

EXPLANATION = 138 ÷ 8 = 17.25. You need one teacher for every 8 students, therefore you would need 18 members of staff in order to cater for 138 students.

Q27. B = $720

EXPLANATION = £1 − 1.60 US dollars. £450 = 450 × 1.60 = $720

Q28. C = West

EXPLANATION = she is facing west, she turns eight right angles clockwise. 1 turn = north, 2 turns = east, 3 turns = south. After eight rotations of 90°, Linda will be facing west.

Q29. C = £161.35

EXPLANATION = 80.4 + 35 + 40 + 490 = 645.40.
645.40 ÷ 4 = 161.35

Q30. D = 80

EXPLANATION = 560 ÷ 7 = 80.

Non-Verbal Reasoning

Non-Verbal Reasoning tests are often used to assess a person's ability to recognise shapes and patterns in regards to formations. The questions appear in diagrammatic and pictorial form, and can be broken up into 3 categories: Abstract, Spatial or Inductive Reasoning.

Non-Verbal Reasoning tests determine how well you can understand and visualise information to solve problems. You need to be able to recognise and identify patterns amongst abstract shapes and images.

Non-Verbal Reasoning tests have become a popular tool for job selection processes, so it is imperative that you get to grips with each question type and know how to answer them.

For psychometric testing, you need to aim for speed as well as accuracy. It is important to be able to undergo these tests with the utmost confidence and composure, in order to work swiftly and effectively throughout the test.

For jobs and careers that involve a practical element, you may be required to sit a Non-Verbal Reasoning test. Non-Verbal Reasoning is also used in school tests, including the 11+ test.

Types of jobs that may require a Non-Verbal Reasoning test are as follows:

- Graduate positions;

- Managerial roles;

- Technical posts.

The types of questions that you will face in the Non-Verbal Reasoning test will vary depending on the type of test you will be sitting. This chapter provides you with a variety of sample questions and explanations, in order to give you a clearer understanding of what to expect.

Such tests may include:

- Determining identical shapes;

- Rotating shapes;

- Reflections of shapes;

- Finding the odd shape;

- Finding the missing shape;

- 3D shapes;

- Coding;

- Shading and colours;

- Number sequences.

Please note, Spatial Reasoning and Abstract Reasoning are very similar tests, but are different. Thus, it is important to know which type of Non-Verbal Reasoning test you will be sitting. However, practising all types of questions can only work in your favour and better your chances at gaining a higher score.

Abstract (or Diagrammatic) – are tests to measure general intelligence. These tests require you to evaluate the rules surrounding the diagrams.

Spatial Reasoning – are tests which work with detailed and complex plans. Often, they rely on mental rotations of shapes.

Now have a go at our sample test!

Question 1

Work out which figure is a top-down 2D view of the 3D shape.

3D Question Figure

2D Views

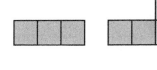 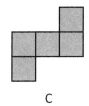

    A   B   C   D

NONE OF THESE

Answer

Question 2

Work out which option fits best in the missing square in order to complete the sequence.

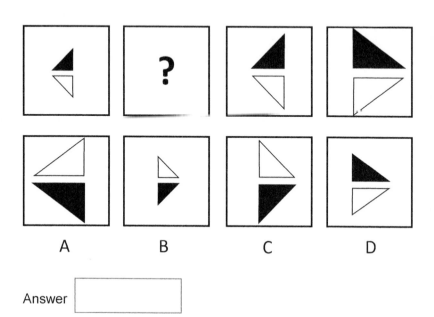

Answer [   ]

Question 3

Work out which 3D shapes from the answer figures are needed to create the Question Figure.

Question Figure

Answer Figures

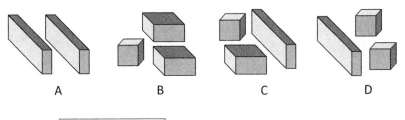

| A | B | C | D |

Answer

Question 4

Work out which 3D shapes from the answer figures are needed to create the Question Figure.

Question Figure

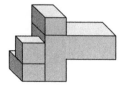

Answer Figures

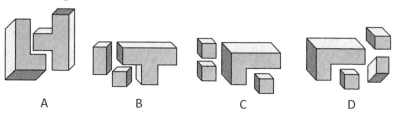

Answer [   ]

Question 5

Work out which option fits best in the missing square in order to complete the sequence.

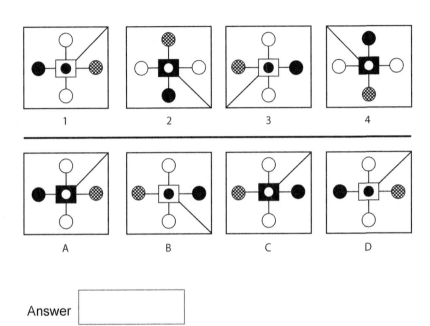

Answer

[   ]

Question 6

Work out which of the cubes can be made from the net.

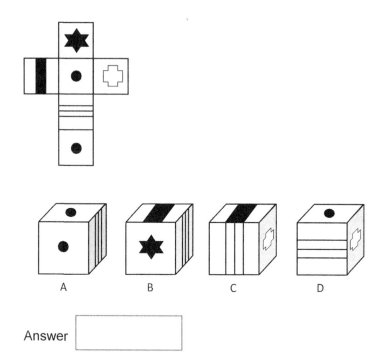

A   B   C   D

Answer [   ]

Question 7

Work out which two shapes are identical. (No rotation or reflection needed). TWO answers required.

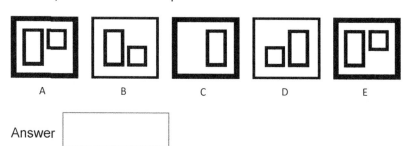

A   B   C   D   E

Answer [   ]

Question 8

Work out which option fits best in the missing square in order to complete the sequence.

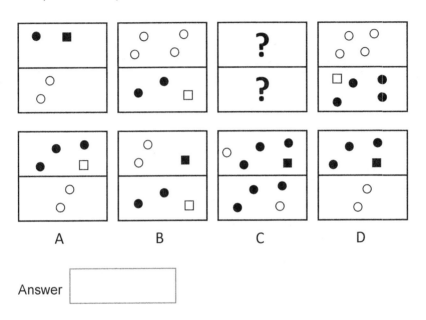

A   B   C   D

Answer

Question 9

Work out which two shapes are identical. (No rotation or reflection needed). TWO answers required.

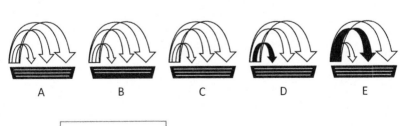

A   B   C   D   E

Answer

Question 10

Work out which two shapes are identical. (No rotation or reflection needed). TWO answers required.

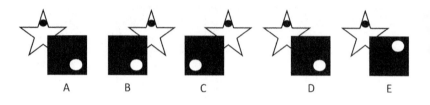

A   B   C   D   E

Answer

Answers

Q1. A

EXPLANATION = a top-down 2D view of the 3D Question Figure would show three squares in a horizontal line.

Q2. D

EXPLANATION = the sequence follows: every even square contains triangles pointing in the right direction, every odd square has triangles pointing in the left direction. The triangles get bigger as the sequence progresses.

Q3.C

EXPLANATION = the Question Figure contains one cube, and two different sized cuboids.

Q4. D

EXPLANATION = the Question Figure contains an 'L' 3D shape, 2 cuboids of the same length, and a cube.

Q5. D

EXPLANATION = within each square the shapes are moving round 90 degrees anti-clockwise as the sequence progresses. You will also notice that the square and inner circle which forms the centre of each shape, are alternating between black and white as the sequence progresses. The diagonal line within each square is moving round clockwise as the sequence progresses.

Q6. D

EXPLANATION = Figure A can be ruled out because the two circles need to be on opposite sides. Figure B can be ruled out because the side with the three lines needs to be a circle instead. Figure C can be ruled out because the 'cross' sign would need to be a circle.

Q7. A and E

EXPLANATION = none of the other shapes are identical. Figures

A and E are identical.

Q8. D

EXPLANATION = starting from the top left box in the first rectangle, the number of dots is one, and also includes a black square. The black square changes colour. One dot is added each time, as the sequence progresses. Starting from the bottom left box in the rectangle, it has two white dots, this follows a zig-zag pattern, of two dots then four dots, two dots then four dots and so forth.

Q9. A and C

EXPLANATION = Figures A and C are the only identical shapes.

Q10. A and D

EXPLANATION = Figures A and D are the only identical shapes.

Offshore Interview

The final stage in the process is for you to sit an interview with a representative from the company. The way this is done will depend very much on the company that you are applying for. You might be asked to take one interview, or you might be asked to sit two interviews. Either way, the main focus of the interview(s) will be on two areas:

- Your understanding of the core competencies, through competency-based questions.

- Your motivation for joining the company, and your personal profile.

If you sit just one interview, then one half of the interview will focus on one side, and the other half will focus on the other. If there are two interviews then each interview will focus on a particular area.

Let's start by looking at the competency-based questions.

Competency Based Interview Questions

Competency-based questions are becoming more and more common in job interviews, and therefore it's essential that you are prepared for how to answer them. A competency-based question is one which focuses on a specific competency, and how you've used the competency in the past. For example, you might be asked:

Give us an example of a time when you have demonstrated good team working skills.

Here, the question takes a very direct approach, directly referencing the competency. However, not all of the questions will be this obvious. You might be asked something like:

Do you see yourself as someone who works well with others? What attributes do you have that make you a good colleague?

This question is asking roughly the same thing, but the question is a bit more subtle, and requires you to think a bit harder about what is being asked. You still need to demonstrate a past example of when you've used that behaviour, and a knowledge of how it applies to the job role.

When answering competency-based questions, it's really important that you do not fall into the trap of providing a 'generic' response that details what you 'would do' if the situation arose, unless of course you have not been in this type of situation before. Instead, you need to say what you DID do.

When responding to situational questions, try to structure your responses in a logical and concise manner. The way to achieve this is to use the 'STAR' method of interview question response construction:

Situation. Start off your response to the interview question by explaining what the 'situation' was and who was involved.

Task. Once you have detailed the situation, explain what the 'task' was, or what needed to be done.

Action. Now explain what 'action' you took, and what action others took. Also explain why you took this particular course of action.

Result. Explain to the panel what you would do differently if the same situation arose again. It is good to be reflective at the end of your responses. This demonstrates a level of maturity and it will also show the interviewer that you are willing to learn from every experience.

Finally, explain what the outcome or result was following your actions and those of others. Try to demonstrate in your response that the result was positive because of the action you took.

The majority of the questions will require you to focus on just on competency. As long as you fully demonstrate the competency that is being asked for in the question, then you will score good marks. You shouldn't try to force extra competencies into your answers. However, if it can be done naturally, then it's always a good idea to demonstrate these. For example, if you are answering a question about leadership, then it's completely normal for other competencies to come up too when recounting your behaviour. Likewise, while the questions will generally focus on just one competency, the interviewers will expect you to show other competencies where possible. For example, if they give you a question about leadership, then it's highly likely that competencies such as communication will need to be factored into your response.

Now, let's look at some sample questions and responses. To help you practice, we've given you a sample question and response to each question.

Q1. Give me an example of a time when you have used your communication skills, in a professional environment.

Sample Response

In my previous role, working at a packing warehouse, I was one of the distribution managers. My role was to coordinate the successful distribution of products, which would be sent out on lorries to customers. Essentially, I was in a supervisory position, ensuring that every member of my team stayed motivated, and that the team was working in a coordinated and efficient manner, as well as making sure that everyone was working to health and safety standards.

One afternoon, just as we were about to close up for the day, I received a phonecall from my boss back at HQ. He asked me whether it would be possible for us to fulfil an extremely large order, before we went home. A customer had complained about a previous shipment, and now they wanted a replacement dispatch as soon as possible. I gathered my team round and explained the situation. Although some of them were reluctant to stick around, as they wanted to go home, I persuaded them to stay by encouraging them to think the customer. I also informed them that they would be paid for their time, if they stayed. To my delight, every member of my team agreed to stay and help.

We had a very short window, to prepare 100 boxes of product, so we needed to work efficiently. I immediately divided the team into groups of 4, and assigned each team a 'group leader'. I conversed with each group leader prior to beginning the task, to ensure they were totally clear on exactly what needed to be done, and to answer any extra questions they might have had.

Once we got to work, I worked my way around the room, ensuring that everyone understood their roles, and motivating them to get this task completed. I routinely checked in with each group leader, to see how they were getting on, and if they were meeting their targets.

I am pleased to say that we managed to complete this task within less than two hours, which was far quicker than I expected. I called my boss to inform him about this and emphasised how brilliantly the team had done to complete the work. He was extremely pleased. I believe that my excellent communication, leadership and motivational skills helped the team to complete this task successfully. Instead of panicking, I took a calm and organised approach, and as a result the job was much easier.

Q2. Can you tell me about a time when you have used your technical knowledge to resolve a problem?

Sample Response

In my previous role, as a systems administrator, I spent a great deal of time working with IT based software. The software in question allowed for better organisation of company events, deadlines and staff-absences/holiday. However, the software was fairly complex.

One month, we had a new member of staff working with us. Her name was Julie. Although Julie was fully competent with IT, she took a little while to master the company software that we used, and as a result made a few initial mistakes. On one such occasion, I noticed that she had become very distressed and agitated, and seemed to be panicking. I immediately approached her, calmly and carefully enquiring about what was wrong. Julie showed me that she had accidentally deleted a key part of the company registry file, and didn't know how to get it back.

The first thing I did was to assure Julie that we would take care of this, and that she did not need to worry or panic. I wanted her to feel at ease, as her panicking certainly would not be beneficial to the situation. My first attempt to bring back the file did not work. However, luckily I had experienced a similar issue before, so I managed to find a way round the problem and restore the file. Julie was delighted with this, and very grateful.

Following this, I sat down with Julie and informed her that I would be happy to help further her understanding of the software that we used. I arranged a time when we could both sit down together and go through the things that she was finding difficult, so that incidents like this could be avoided in future.

Eventually, with my help, Julie became proficient at using the company software – and has now progressed to the level where she is a manager within the company.

I believe that my patient and calm approach, coupled with my technical expertise and experience, helped to solve this problem and improve the company in the long term.

Q3. Can you give me an example of a time when you have assumed responsibility for dealing with a difficult problem?

Sample Response

In my previous role, I worked as a team leader at a catering company. The company had a great reputation, and are well-known nationally. Our company would be paid to organise the catering for parties and events, with different events being given to different teams within the organisation.

As one of the team leaders, my role was to oversee the management of any projects that my team was given. This included making sure that the budget was kept to, motivating staff to perform at their best, and giving my team instructions on how we should allocate our resources. In order to help me manage the team, I had assigned a sub-team leader, named Michelle. Michelle would essentially act as my deputy, and would be given responsibility for taking key decisions.

On the day in question, we were preparing for an event in Wolverhampton. The event in question was a big birthday party. I sent my team to the venue to help start setting up, whilst I met with the person who was running the event, just to crosscheck on key elements such as time, and food allergy requirements. When I arrived at the venue, I found that two members of the team were engaged in a furious debate. One of them was Michelle. Voices were being raised and things were getting extremely heated. This was attracting the attention of the venue staff, who looked extremely unimpressed by the situation.

I quickly stepped across, and asked Michelle and the other team member to calm down and come with me outside, so that we could resolve this. I then calmly and professionally asked them to explain what the issue was. Michelle explained to me that the team member in question was refusing to obey her instructions. She had asked him to lay out a series of fish pasties across the table on the right-hand side, but he had refused. Upon hearing this, the team member furiously interrupted. He said that we shouldn't be serving fish pasties, because some attendees would be allergic to fish. He referred to Michelle in extremely demeaning terms.

Having spoken with the event manager, I was fully aware of all allergy requirements – and none of the attendees were allergic to fish.

After listening to the complaints, I first addressed the team member. I explained to him that the way he had spoken to Michelle was completely unacceptable, and that even if she had made a mistake then this would not be okay. I then explained to him that he was in fact wrong, and there were no attendees who were allergic. To back this up, I showed him the event listing, which contained the details of all known allergies.

Once the team member saw this, he acknowledged that he had made a mistake, and apologised profusely to Michelle. He begged me not to fire him. Michelle immediately accepted his apology, and informed him that mistakes happen, and that the important thing is to move forward and resolve this. I was happy with this, and authorised the team member to get back to work.

Following this, I spoke to Michelle and informed her that I was pleased with how she dealt with the situation, and that she was doing a great job.

Q4. Can you give me an example of a time when you have demonstrated your personal discipline? This can be mental or physical.

Sample Response

A few years ago, I decided that I wanted to raise money for charity. There was a local marathon taking place within the next few months, so I thought, 'What better way to raise money?' I must say that I was not in the best physical shape at that time, so the run would also benefit my physical health.

Obviously, I was in no condition to run a marathon, so first I needed to train. In order to do this, I drew myself up a detailed schedule, listing all of the exercises I would do, when I would do them, and how long I would do them for. I accounted for 3 months of training, which I hoped would put me in good condition for the run.

At first, it was incredibly hard. I hadn't exercised much for a while, and so body found it tough. I was frequently exhausted and it took all my mental and physical strength just to keep going. But little by little, it got easier and easier, and I even started enjoying it. It was just a case of getting through the early stages, where the amount of work I was doing was so unfamiliar to me. Initially, I had to pace myself, because I was trying to do too much too fast.

As a result of my preparation, I managed to get fit enough to complete the marathon, and I finished the whole thing – raising over two thousand pounds for charity.

I don't believe that I could have managed this without good mental discipline. I had to use all of my willpower to keep pushing myself forward, and overcome the physical hurdles – but ultimately I managed this, and the end result was hugely positive.

Q5. Tell me about a time when you have used your organisational skills to good effect.

Sample Response

Whilst working for my previous company as a member of the events team, I was part of the group responsible for managing and organising company conferences. In order to do this, we would have to make contact with the owners of the venue, as well as our client, and negotiate factors such as cost, availability and catering.

The event in question was to be a large-scale conference. Our client was an international refurbishment company, who were running the conference in order to enhance their business network. There were going to be over 500 people attending this conference, from all around the world, so it was essential that we got it right!

The first thing I did was to contact the manager of our client company. I asked him to provide me with a list of every single attendee, where they were travelling from, and whether they would have any special requirements. After the manager sent this through, I split the list into 5 separate parts – with 100 people being sent to 5 different teams within our department. I felt that this was the best approach to managing such a huge number of people. At all times, we liased with the other teams, to make sure everyone was on the right track.

Next, I contacted another department in our company, who were in charge of dealing with issues such as reviews and feedback. I asked them to provide me with the feedback we'd had on our past events, so that I could make sure we did the same things right, and improved on any weak areas. Once they provided me with this list, I made it a priority to improve on the areas which had received negative feedback.

Following the event, which was a huge success, I arranged a meeting with the manager of our client company, to get their thoughts on how the event was run. I wanted to make sure that we worked with this client, in a collaborative fashion, to run future events. The client seemed very happy with how the event was run, and provided us with sustained feedback – which we took into account for the future.

Q6. Tell me about a time when you have shown desire and commitment to improve your skills.

Sample Response

I currently work as a telecommunications engineer and I have been doing this job for nine years now. I am very well qualified, and can carry out the tasks that form part of my job description both professionally and competently. However, with the introduction of wireless telecommunications I started to feel a little bit out of my depth.

Wireless telecommunications provide telephone, Internet, data, and other services to customers through the transmission of signals over networks of radio towers. The signals are transmitted through an antenna directly to customers, who use devices such as mobile phones and mobile computers to receive, interpret, and send information. I knew very little about this section of the industry and decided to ask my line manager for an appraisal. During the appraisal I raised my concerns about my lack of knowledge in this area and she agreed to my request for continuing professional training in this important area.

As part of my role, I often have to communicate directly with customers, dealing with their issues and queries. Given that I was learning a variety of new things, I felt that it was my responsibility to make sure that I was fully equipped to help all of our customers out to the best of my ability.

Along with the new training that I would be provided with, I also sought out advice from my line manager on the best way to link my new skills with great customer service. Together, we ran through a plan of action that would allow me to do so.

I was soon booked on a training course which was modular in nature and took seven weeks to complete. During the training I personally ensured that I studied hard, followed the curriculum and checked with the course tutor periodically to assess my performance and act on any feedback they offered.

At the end of the training I received a distinction for my efforts. I now felt more comfortable in my role at work and I also started to apply for different positions within the company that involved wireless technology. For the last six months I have been working in the wireless telecommunications research department for my company and have excelled in this new area of expertise.

Q7. Give me an example of a time when you have demonstrated your awareness of health and safety.

Sample Response

Whilst working in my previous position as a sales person, I was the duty manager for the day, as my manager had gone sick. It was the week before Christmas and the shop was very busy.

During the day the fire alarm went off, and I started to ask everybody to evacuate the shop, which is our company policy. The alarm has gone off in the past but the normal manager usually lets people stay in the shop whilst he finds out if it's a false alarm.

This was a difficult situation because the shop was very busy, nobody wanted to leave and my shop assistants were disagreeing with me in my decision to evacuate the shop. Some of the customers were becoming irate as they were in the changing rooms at the time. The customers were saying that it was appalling that they had to evacuate the shop and that they would complain to the head office about it. The sales staff were trying to persuade me to keep everybody inside the shop, and saying that it was most probably a false alarm as usual. I was determined to evacuate everybody from the shop for safety reasons, and would not allow anybody to deter me from my aim. The safety of my staff and customers was at the forefront of my mind, even though it wasn't at theirs.

Whilst remaining calm and in control, I shouted at the top of my voice that everybody was to leave, even though the sound of the alarm was reducing the impact of my voice. I then had to instruct my staff to walk around the shop and tell everybody to leave whilst we investigated the problem. I had to inform one member of staff that disciplinary action would be taken against him if he did not co-operate. Eventually, after I kept persisting, everybody began to leave the shop. I then went outside with my members of staff, took a roll call and awaited the Fire Brigade to arrive.

At first I felt a little apprehensive and under pressure, but was determined not to move from my position, as I knew 100% that it was the right one. I was disappointed that my staff did not initially help me, but the more I persisted the more confident I became. Eventually the Fire Brigade showed up, and they discovered that there was in fact a small fire at the back of the store. Luckily nobody was harmed, but the consequences could have been severe if I hadn't got everyone out.

This was the first time I had been the manager of the shop so I felt that this situation tested my courage and determination. By remaining calm I was able to deal with the situation far more effectively. I now felt that I had the courage to manage the shop better and had proven to myself that I was capable of dealing with difficult situations. I had learnt that staying calm under pressure improves your chances of a successful outcome dramatically.

Motivations and Values Questions

Along with competency-focused questions, it's highly likely that you will be asked motivations and values type questions. These are the 'regular' type interview questions that you might expect. For example, 'Why do you want to work for this company?' 'What motivated you to apply for working offshore?' or 'Do you think you can cope for long periods without your family?'

The best way to answer these types of questions is to be honest. However, there's work to be done before the interview. In pretty much every single offshore interview that you have, you'll be asked about the company specific, and what it is about them that appeals to you. This means that you need to have conducted research BEFORE the interview, (although really you should be doing this before you even apply!) so that you can answer these questions in an eloquent and capable fashion.

Let's take a look at a few motivations and values questions. We'll show you the type of questions you might expect, and give you some advice on how to answer them.

Q1. Tell me about yourself.

This is the classic opening question, and should be pretty easy to answer. The key to answering this question is to keep your answer focused and structured. Don't go off on a tangent, telling the interviewer about where you were born, where you grew up, etc. This isn't relevant. When the interview says, 'Tell me about yourself' they want to find out the following:

- What type of person you are.

- What type of work you've done in the past.

- How you've come to apply for this job.

When answering this question, think about the competencies. Using phrases like 'hardworking' 'passionate' 'dedicated' 'organised' will really go a long way to showing the interviewer that you are the type of person they are looking for. Ideally, you should keep this answer fairly short and concise. As interesting as you might be, the interviewer doesn't need to hear your life story – only the parts which are relevant to the role!

Bonus Tip: When you talk about the type of work you've done in the past, try and find ways to link this to the position you're applying for. This will show the interviewer that you have the experience they need.

Q2. Why do you want to work for this company in particular?

Here's where your research will be really important. The bottom line is this: companies want to know that you've looked into them, and they like to be flattered! So, tell them what it is that you like. Be specific. Go onto their website and look around. Search for the company ethos and the values/principles that mean the most to the organisation.

For example, the company might put particular emphasis on caring for the environment, and ensuring their work is environmentally safe. If this matches with your own philosophy, then make sure you say so! The more detail you can show, the better.

Bonus Tip: Don't go too far! Most companies enjoy being flattered, but it's obvious if you are just exaggerating. Try to keep your praise realistic and relevant.

Q3. How do you think you'd cope with being away from your family/friends?

This is a common question which comes up during offshore interviews. It's extremely important to the employer that candidates know what they're getting into – as it would be disastrous for them to give you the job, only for you to quit within a week as you can't cope with being away from your loved ones. Offshore work isn't for everyone, and this is part of the reason. To be honest, if your answer to this question is, 'I wouldn't be able to cope' then you probably shouldn't be interviewing for the job – because that's the reality of working on an offshore rig.

While you need to assure the interviewer that you can cope, don't go too far. You still need to show them that you are a human being, and not a heartless robot! So, a great answer will be something along the lines of:

'Yes, I would. I know it will be difficult, but I have discussed the idea of me working offshore with my family, and they fully support my decision. Although of course I will miss them, I'm confident that we can manage.'

This response should fill the interviewer with confidence that you are aware of the difficulties. If you can tell them that you have discussed it with your family then that's even better – because it's not uncommon for families to veto the career move.

Q4. What do you do to keep yourself fit and healthy?

This is an important question, because working on an offshore rig is a physically demanding and difficult role. Therefore, if you are applying for a job such as roustabout, then the interviewers will want to know that you are up to the task. Again, it would be disastrous if they gave you the job, only for you to quit a week later because you can't cope with the physical demands. Your answer to this question doesn't have to be really long or in-depth, just give them an honest response. Tell them exactly what you do to stay in shape, for example:

'I go to the gym two times a week, and on Wednesdays and Saturdays I play for a men's football team.'

On top of this, make sure you show them that fitness is important to you. This will impress the interviewers more than if you just exercise for the sake of staying in shape. For example:

'Fitness is really important to me. Staying in good physical shape doesn't just impact your body, but your mind too. I understand that working offshore requires a great deal of physical and mental exertion, and I'm more than up to the task.'

Q5. Are you an ambitious person? Where do you see yourself in ten years' time?

When an offshore company hires you, they aren't just hiring you to 'fill a gap'. Even if you are applying for an entry level position, such as roustabout, the company want you to progress. They will be looking for candidates with the drive and ambition to learn new skills and develop, leading them on to bigger and better things within the organisation. For example, if you are a roustabout then you can train to become a crane operator, or progress on to more specialised fields such as driller. So, showing the interviewer that you are ambitious and want to improve will really help. Again, you don't have to go too far, but a realistic and sensible response could be something like this:

'Yes, I am ambitious, and I would really like to progress within your company. When I researched online, I discovered that there are a wealth of opportunities available for workers within your organisation, and this was hugely appealing to me. I am not someone who is satisfied with being 'bottom of the ladder' – I always want to better my skills and learn new ways of making myself more valuable to the company.'

Basically, you need to show the interviewer that you are someone with a drive to succeed and improve. On top of this, the interviewer will want to know that you are 'in it for the long haul'. By this, we mean that they obviously don't want to hire someone who will leave within the space of a year. So, make sure you tell them that! Endeavour to persuade the interviewer that you are dedicated to the role, and want to rise within the organisation.

Other motivations and values questions

Obviously, the five questions above aren't the only ones you'll see! There are a huge number of interview questions that could come up, including:

-    What is your biggest strength?

-    What is your biggest weakness?

- How do you think you would deal with being managed by someone else?

- How well can you work to deadlines?

- What does the term 'health and safety' mean to you?

- How do you feel about travelling?

You might also be asked, 'Do you have any questions for me?' If you hear this, then make sure you endeavour to ask some constructive questions. Failing to ask questions could be interpreted by the interviewer as a lack of interest/enthusiasm, which is certainly not the impression you want to give at the end of the interview! Questions that you could ask include:

- What are the opportunities for progression within this company?

- What type of training will I receive?

- What type of facilities are available on board the platform?

- Do you have any concerns about my ability to do the job?

You have now reached the end of your guide to Offshore Work, and no doubt you feel more prepared to tackle the selection process

We hope you have found this guide an invaluable insight, and understand the expectations regarding your assessments.

For any type of test, we believe there are a few things to remember in order to better your chances and increase your overall performance.

REMEMBER – THE THREE Ps!

1. Preparation. This may seem relatively obvious, but you will be surprised by how many people fail just because they lacked preparation and knowledge regarding the selection process. You want to do your utmost to guarantee the best possible chance of succeeding. Be sure to conduct as much preparation prior to your assessments and interview, to ensure you are fully aware and 100% prepared to complete them successfully. Not only will practising guarantee to better your chances of successfully passing, but it will also make you feel at ease by providing you with the knowledge and know-how to pass, and secure a job in the industry.

2. Perseverance. You are far more likely to succeed at something if you continuously set out to achieve it. Everybody comes across times whereby they are setback or find obstacles in the way of their goals. The important thing to remember when this happens, is to use those setbacks and obstacles as a way of progressing. It is what you do with your past experiences that helps to determine your success in the future. If you fail at something, consider 'why' you have failed. This will allow you to improve and enhance your performance for next time.

3. Performance. Your performance will determine whether or not you are likely to succeed. Attributes that are often associated with performance are self-belief, motivation and commitment. Self-belief is important for anything you do in life. It allows you to recognise your own abilities and skills and believe that you can do well. Believing that you can do well is half the battle! Being fully motivated and committed is often difficult for some people, but we can assure you that, nothing is gained without hard work and determination. If you want to succeed, you will need to put in that extra time and hard work!

Good luck with your Offshore Worker application. We wish you the best of luck with all your future endeavours!

The how2become team

The How2Become Team

WANT FURTHER HELP PASSING THE SELECTION PROCESS? CHECK OUT OUR OTHER GUIDES:

FOR MORE INFORMATION CHECK OUT THE FOLLOWING:
WWW.HOW2BECOME.COM

Get Access To
FREE
Psychometric
Tests

www.PsychometricTestsOnline.co.uk

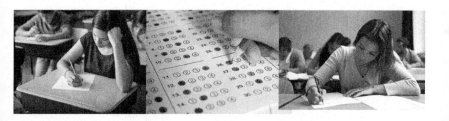